MY BROTHERS AND I

A Sequel to

HERDBOY OF HUNGARY

MY
BROTHERS
AND I

Written and Illustrated by

ALEXANDER FINTA

Holiday House, New York

TO MY DEAR WIFE

CATHERINE FINTA

Copyright, 1940, by Holiday House, Inc.

Designed by Helen Gentry

Contents

Foreword

MY DEAR MOTHER *told me the story many times, how when I was a very young man, only about three days old, I got a slap in the face. It was from my father. He saw that during the solemn ceremony of baptism I was having a deep sleep. I was not paying the slightest attention to anything about me when his slap woke me.*

"Boy," he said, "keep your eyes open whenever anything important is happening to you."

Since that time, I've kept my eyes open. If, in our daily escapades, my brothers and I saw severe consequences about to descend, we kept our eyes open and found the nearest exit, and I was usually the first to find that remedy for saving my skin.

I was a good student in school, diligent in learning and quick to finish my tasks. But it was agony for me to listen to repetition of any kind, and those lessons which had been easy for me bored me as I listened to the other boys in the class struggling to repeat them for our master. This was the cause of many of my misdeeds in my early school years, and was why I was expelled from that school at the age of nine.

My father thought, wrongly, that it was the bad companionship of older boys, and took me far away from home and friends to work on my uncle's ranch. In Hungary, this ranch is called Ecseg, and there I learned to herd cattle and horses, and to ride my own horse, Mocskos.

Though I liked being a herdboy, the life was monotonous, and I filled in the time with studying the birds which lived in great numbers in the swamps of the region. It was my good luck to find many rare specimens of nests and eggs and feathers of birds little known then, and the fame of my collection came to the ears of Mr. Otto Herman, an internationally known ornithologist. (It was he who devised the law, internationally obeyed, defending the migratory birds.)

Mr. Herman came to Ecseg to study birds, and I was able to help him so well that when he returned to the city, he recommended me for a scholarship in the Gymnasium of Nagyvarad. At the same time that he was be-

friending me in town, I was getting into trouble back on the ranch. I had teased my Aunt Zsuzsa's donkey, Crinolin, until it dashed off into the Puszta with her and caused no end of trouble. In terror of what my uncle might do, I mounted Mocskos and ran away, ending my career as a herdboy. After a night of wandering, I drove the horse back in the direction of my uncle's ranch, and started home on foot, which is where this story starts.

SOME
MISHAPS OF MOVING

Chapter One

WHEN I turned the knob of our front door, I thought, "What excuse can I give my parents for leaving Uncle's farm so suddenly?"

I did not have much time to consider the matter because one of my sisters at that moment spied me, and calling "Sandor, here's Sandor come home!" roused the whole family. In another moment I was surrounded by the lively, chattering throng. Throng it was, for I had six brothers and two sisters, and my father was big enough for two people and made up for the slenderness of my mother.

They gave me no chance to wonder at the good fortune of finding them all at home, for at once they began telling me, now one and now another, about a letter. At first I could not understand what it was all about, and I looked confusedly at each in turn. At last my father spoke sternly: "Hush, all!"

When the room was quiet, he explained. "Just now, son, a letter came from the Minister of Education of Hungary. Here it is." He held up the long official envelope. "You needn't read it till later, but I will tell you what it says—that Mr. Otto Herman has brought your name to the attention of the Minister, recommending you for a scholarship in the Gymnasium." I gasped, for the Gymnasium was the classical high school of Hungary, and far beyond the dreams of a poor family like our own.

My father interrupted himself long enough to ask, "Who is this Mr. Otto Herman, Sandor?"

I looked about the room in pride. I, who had come home wondering how to confess my disgrace, was the center of attention. Ten pairs of eyes were fixed upon me. I spoke slowly so that none might miss a word. "Mr. Otto Herman is the most famous ornithologist in Hungary. The last two summers on the plains of the Puszta, I helped him gather birds' nests and eggs, and to make scientific researches." The big words rolled off my tongue so glibly that my mother pulled in her chin in surprise. "He sent me books, but I never expected anything like this. What else does the letter say, Father?"

"The Minister promised a scholarship of two hundred pengoes in the Gymnasium of Nagyvarad. That is a lot of money, son." My father spoke solemnly. In our little village it was indeed a great sum; although it amounted to but eighty dollars in American money, it was enough to keep even so large a family as ours for a long time. "We were just about to send to your uncle's ranch for you, and we were deciding which of us should go. And now, like a miracle, here you are!" My father put his arms about me, and almost crushed me in his strong embrace.

We had a real holiday. I was the hero, and my brothers and sisters kept me talking the whole day long. Immediately after supper I fell into a sleep which lasted more than twenty-four hours. Mother told me later how she tried over and over again to waken me, and frightened at last, called my father. He merely looked at me and said, "Let him rest."

When on the evening of the next day I woke, I saw that the friendly smile was gone from my father's face. He watched me with his serious eyes full of questions. I knew I must tell him what had happened. And I thought perhaps it might go easier with me while I was still weak from exhaustion and hunger. I propped myself up with pillows, and my father sat on the edge of the bed.

"Now, Sandor, why did you leave the Puszta?" he asked.

I felt about in my mind for some way of telling the story which would make it more acceptable. My poor mother, who was standing beside him, made me more nervous than ever, for I knew she was fearful that this time I was in worse trouble than usual. After long hesitation, and "Come, come, son, tell us!" from my father, I haltingly told my story.

"Aunt Zsuzsa was forever torturing me," I began. "She complained that I did not wash the herdsmen's dinner pot clean, and that I was no good in the kitchen, and she beat me often with her umbrella." I rubbed my head in memory.

"Yes, yes, but what did you do?"

When I told how I had put burning cotton into her donkey's ears and how Aunt Zsuzsa had caught her feet in the laundry sacks fastened to the saddle and been carried off on the donkey into the Puszta, I thought I saw a faint smile behind my father's mustache. He covered it quickly with his hand, but it gave me confidence to go on, and soon I had related the whole tale, how fearful I had been of what my uncle, in his terrible anger, might do, and how I had run away from the ranch on my horse, Mocskos. And then, as big a boy as I was, my lips trembled and my eyes filled with tears as I told how I had at last sent away my companion of three years by striking her across her beautiful eyes and starting her back in the direction of my uncle's ranch.

By this time the whole family was gathered about, listening, and I saw my sisters and my mother wipe their eyes at this point, and even my father's face softened. I told then how I had gone to sleep, there on the side of the road, and turned homeward when I awoke. It was not long before a wagon which was headed for the fair in Nagyvarad, picked me up and helped me along the way, almost to the very door of our home.

"It was fate," I ended, "which made my Aunt Zsuzsa catch her foot in the sack, and so fate brought about my downfall."

Although my father had an entirely different opinion concerning fate and my aunt, he did not scold me at once, but left that until he should have adjusted the whole matter with Uncle Miklos. Meanwhile, he spent a great deal of time smoking hard and pacing the room silently. This was a sign that he was thinking deeply.

All the next day we stole about as silently as possible, so as not to disturb him. At last he told us what he had been considering—how to manage the further education of all of us. He had made up his mind to take the whole family and move to the city where we could all go to school. It did not seem fair to the other children, he said, that I should have an education and they be left without an equal opportunity.

Furthermore, he looked upon the two hundred pengoes as so great a sum of money that with it and a little good luck all his sons of school age (there were five of us then), might have some higher education. At that time, because of the Russo-Turkish war, a severe economic depression paralyzed the whole country, and my father's sudden decision to leave the village of Puspoki, where there was little opportunity of earning a living to support so large a family, seemed sound enough. In the city he would have a better chance of getting a position.

Father was a man of prompt action. "We need not waste our time in further delay," he said. "We shall move to the city at once."

All of us thought that a splendid idea. The Fintas immediately began to wrap and pack their belongings.

Each one had his pets, and all those must go too; our pigeons, our rabbits, the wild birds in their cages, the geese, ducks, hens, and even some little pigs which were great favorites of Gergely, my brother. The front room was piled high with our bundles and packages, the farmyard stacked with cages and pens. All was in readiness. Father hired an ox-cart and driver, and we went about saying goodbye to our neighbors. They were almost as happy over our leaving as we were ourselves. Nine growing children were something to be rid of!

Our destination was Nagyvarad, one of the oldest cities of Hungary, and so famous for its learning, its art, and its culture that it was commonly called "the Hungarian's Rome." But even more famous was its long and colorful past. Standing on the Transylvanian frontier, it had been an outpost of civilization for hundreds of years, protecting Europe from the invasions of Mongols, Tartars, and Moslems. Its strange architecture and the zigzag pattern of its streets were the result of building for defense, not beauty. At one time there had been as many armories as churches, with columns of soldiers marching through the streets, or parading in the public squares, until the whole city seemed overflowing with bustle and excitement.

Even now, the farmers held an open-air market every second day, and their bright embroidered cloaks and feathered hats, their carts heaped with their gay wares, made the city as vivid as a fair. It was a place to amaze and astonish the simple country folk. We children could hardly contain our wonder.

My father and mother, however, were familiar with the sights and sounds and smells of that ancient city and drove directly to the end of town where the humbler people had their quarters. Here they hoped to find a home for us. It was not so easy, alas. With seven boys, two girls, and a cartload of pets, we drove from house to house seeking a place to live. When the landlords learned, after asking the usual questions, that the family was composed of eleven members, besides many pigeons and rabbits and pigs, we were refused in every street and at every house. Father at first would not be discouraged, but by evening he admitted with resignation, "There is no place for us in the city."

"Try some place else, Father," we coaxed. We did not want

to return to our village to be laughed at. "Try one house more."

He agreed; but the landlord would rent his quarters only at an exorbitant price, and just to the family, with no room for the animals at any price. When Father turned to us with, "What about leaving out the animals?" such a shout of dismay went up that he could do nothing but turn away.

The cart, piled sky-high with our belongings and cages, moved slowly, drawn by the hungry oxen. It must have seemed a ridiculous sight to the city boys who had followed us about all day long in the narrow winding streets. Toward evening, an undesirable crowd drew around us, asking useless questions by the hundreds. At first we answered, but when we found that they only meant to make fun of us, we tried to

pay no attention. At last their taunts grew unbearable; we five boys pulled out the daggers we wore in our belts and before anyone could stop us we were in the midst of a hot fight. It might have had a sad ending if our father had not kept his head and commanded us to stop. Even the street boys recognized the authority in his voice, and slunk away.

Father, irritated now, had about decided to turn back to the village from which we had started, when someone called his name. It was an old friend, who, attracted by the crowd, had stopped to see what was happening, and had recognized us. He offered to help us.

The menagerie, he thought, was the biggest hindrance to our finding a home in the city. "Why not," he proposed, "move to some place out of town, where your children can feed their pets and care for them until they are disposed of? I know of an abandoned brick factory which might do temporarily."

Father agreed that that was an excellent idea, and with his friend he left to find the owner of the factory.

While Father was gone, poor Mother tried to feed us, and we tried to feed our pets, which made a free show for the street crowd. They made comments on our every move, and impertinent suggestions. If we had not been so tired, we might have had another fight on our hands.

It was late when Father returned, but he brought good news.

"I have taken a fine place, just outside the city. They do not mind how many boys, nor how many pets."

Weariness was forgotten. We started at once toward the old brick factory, which seemed to us the Promised Land. In the darkness it was not an easy place to find, and though we had started out so eagerly we were soon stumbling half asleep behind the ox-cart, trying to keep our heavy eyes on the cages of our pets. The high price offered by some in the crowd who had followed us all day made us fear that our animals might be stolen. We did not know that what they had said had been only to make fun of us. It seemed forever before we reached our destination.

In that deserted neighborhood no one could give us exact information about the building we were looking for. Father was able to locate it only by trying each door until he found one into which the key fitted. It was midnight when he swung open the door and called to us, "I've found it. Drive in the oxen."

In the dark we did not see how narrow was the bridge of boards which connected the road with the yard of the factory. We started over; the oxen were across; but the cart wheels on one side slid off the boards, and the whole cart upset into the deep ditch!

Such an outcry as filled the air! The grunt of pigs, the frightened squawks of all manner of birds—pigeons and hens, ducks and wild things trapped in falling cages. "The birds will all be killed," I cried. "My pigs are running off into the darkness," shouted Gergely. "And the rabbits! And the ducks! They'll get away!" Our sleepiness was gone in an instant. Each one tried to save his own pets, and not even Father with his sternest voice could restore order.

Our parents managed at last to rekindle the fire which had been smouldering on the edge of the ditch, and by its light we unloaded our cargo. We clambered in and out of the ditch, carrying the cages to a place of safety. First one and then an-

other of us would begin weeping afresh as we found new dis-
asters. Only the owner of the oxen looked happy, and he because he knew that as soon as the cart was unloaded he could
drive it home.

Father helped us, and soon every cage was indoors. We ran
about the rooms, counting the animals that were left, and trying to reckon our losses. All the rabbits had escaped, all the
pigeons had flown away into the dark; there remained only
three little black pigs and some of the smallest of the wild
birds.

We begged Father to let us go and hunt for the escaped
animals at once, but he forbade any further search that night.

Mother and Father spent the whole night trying to make
the factory livable, and when we woke early the next morning, our old furniture sitting about in the rooms made the place
seem already quite like home.

We started out at once to look for the lost pets. Soon, to
our joy, we found our pigeons on the roof of a half-ruined
building. With coaxing and food we knew we could get them
to come back to us. We recognized one of our rabbits hopping
in a neighboring field, but the grass was too long and too wet
to walk in easily, so we gave him up, for that day at any rate.
And as we went home to breakfast we consoled ourselves with
the thought that we had caught rare wild birds before. We
could catch them again.

UNCLE ESZENYI
TEACHER EXTRAORDINARY

Chapter Two

IT WAS late September when we moved to the city, and the school year had already begun. So the very morning after our arrival Father said to us, "Put on your best clothes. We are going to find out whether or not you are to go to the Gymnasium. I do not want you to lose any more time from your studies."

Mother helped us into our finest garments, which were the picturesque ones of the rural boys of Hungary. I wore black boots, a richly embroidered coat, a hat decorated with its bustard feather, and about my neck I looped the long whip that a herder of horses might use. To top off all this elegance, I had a small dark-red terracotta pipe, with a short stem of cherry wood, and a tobacco pouch as colorful as my coat, from which hung a piece of flint and a bit of steel. These the Hungarian, who is a heavy smoker, wears proudly at his linen girdle.

Father started forth with his five sons of school age, all in their best. He carried the letter from the Minister of Education, and with it as a talisman we hoped for a lucky fate. In spite of the letter we were all a little nervous, however, and soon after we had called goodbye to Mother, Father and I began to smoke feverishly, so that before long a cloud of smoke marked our passage. All in line, one behind another, we neared the city like a small triumphal procession, with the swift-fading smoke from our pipes billowing out like banners.

Father had to ask the way frequently, and when at last we found the Gymnasium he went inside to inquire for the right persons to whom to present our case. He was not gone long, and when he reappeared in the doorway, he said, "Come. They know all about Sandor, and are expecting us."

The Gymnasium of Nagyvarad belonged in those days to the Premonstratensian monks, who are famous for their educational system, and whose order in Hungary is very wealthy. We were conducted at once to the principal of the school, a round-faced father with a friendly smile. When he heard why we had come, he immediately called several other teachers into the room. They were all interested in me, but curious to know why Father had brought five boys with him when the letter from the Secretary of Education clearly mentioned my name and no other.

Father answered clearly and shortly. "I do not want one of my sons to be better educated than the others. If one goes to the Gymnasium, they all go. If they can't—well, there will be no further education here."

Such stout resolution pleased the monks, but they asked if they might test me before they decided any further. They wanted to learn if I were as able and intelligent as the old scientist, Mr. Otto Herman, had said. As they prepared to examine me I grew more and more nervous, and began to smoke.

"Is that necessary?" asked the principal.

"It may help with his answers," replied my father seriously.

They nodded their permission, and soon I had a thick cloud around me, which only lightened when I stopped to listen to the first question. My feelings eased as I gave the first prompt reply. Then, after each question, I would smoke until I had composed my answer, give it, and then with a fine long puff

would clear the air around me. Father and my younger brothers watched me with pride. Father would observe me closely, as if his own intentness might help. Then, when he saw I was capable of answering the question, he would lift his pipe high and wait with patience. The teachers seemed as pleased by my knowledge as they were amused by our manners.

The examination lasted a long time, but at last the principal turned to my father, and declared that, considering my age, my abilities in science were quite remarkable. He said that they were willing to take me into an advanced class, but at the same time make it possible for me to improve my knowledge of Latin and other languages, in which I was quite deficient. Also, I must promise to learn the principles of the Roman Catholic faith, for it was one of the rules of their order that they may not teach a boy who is not willing to accept their religion. My father was shocked to hear this. After a moment or two of consideration, he gave his answer.

"Sir, my sons are Calvinists. They shall not have an education which demands that they turn Catholic, and no scholarship would be acceptable on those terms. I shall work hard and my boys too, and we shall get an education while we breathe with a free conscience. Goodbye to you! My sons, we must go."

The next day Father tried to register us in the regular Gymnasium, but because the school year had already begun, they would not take us. We might try again next year, they said.

"There is nothing left to do," Father said, "but to try the public school. You, Sandor, will have to be content with the upper class."

And so it was arranged. The principal of the school was my teacher. He was well known not only in the city of Nagyvarad, but in the whole country roundabout. He had taught three generations of boys, and was just completing his sixtieth year of teaching. His name was Alexander Eszenyi, but according to custom we called him simply "Uncle Eszenyi." Among ourselves we spoke of him as "Eszi ba"—Eszenyi means "one of great knowledge" but Eszi means "big eater."

He was a stern man, whose face was red as much from violent temper as from his fondness for the rich wines of Hungary. They did say of him that his pleasant voice when he sang came from his having drunk so much wine for so many years!

He was so famous as a teacher that many noble families, when a child of theirs failed in another school, brought him to Uncle Eszenyi, who had no failures. Either a boy learned, or he left school—there was no middle road!

Uncle Eszenyi had won his great reputation long years before. As a young teacher, he took great delight in writing songs. He had never been really successful, however, as a poet, so he amused himself by collecting folk songs, rewriting and revising them. He lived in a part of the country where there were splendid chances for this, for the city of Nagyvarad is at the gateway to Transylvania where, in Uncle Eszenyi's younger days, all wagoners met to exchange the goods they carried. That was in the time before railroads, and everything was transported to and from Vienna by wagons which went far beyond Nagyvarad in their journeyings.

These wagoners were generally good singers, and Uncle Eszenyi frequently visited the inns and camping grounds where they stopped for the night, treating each other freely and singing lustily—which was all good business. Once he heard a song which he rearranged so well that it became popular through Hungary, not only among the common people but among the nobility as well. At the coronation of Franz Joseph in Budapest it was the song written by Uncle Eszenyi which opened the court ball. It was called "Csardas," and this is how it went:

"Kis szekeres, nagy szekeres
Mind megissza amit keres.
A lovaval mig oda jár,
Száz forintnak a végére jár."

Which in English means:

"Little wagoner, big wagoner,
They always drink what they earn.
Before they ride off on their horses again
They spend every penny they own."

The song, played at the ball by the best gypsy band in Budapest, won so much attention that the young king asked the
name of the composer. A search was begun, and the composer
was found—a humble public school teacher named Eszenyi.
The superiors of the school district immediately appointed
him principal of the school in Nagyvarad. But the distinction
that had come to him only whetted his ambition to become a
poet. As he grew older, it became his hobby to compose patriotic words to the innumerable drinking songs which flower
like the grape blossoms in that part of Hungary. Another
hobby of this queer old schoolmaster was to get his pupils to
compose rhymes. Each morning he would ask for them, and
if one of us had a good one ready, he was praised and for
that day was the hero of the class. Or if one of the boys missed
a lesson, or was caught in some mischief, he could always
escape by quickly composing a rhyme.

The first day after our registration, Gergely, Istvan, Arpad,
Samuel, and myself, set out for school, but the streets were
so confusing that we lost our way and were very late—a grave
offence in the eyes of Uncle Eszenyi. In vain I offered the ex-

cuse of not knowing the way to come. He told me, as the oldest, to stand with the other boys who were waiting special tasks as punishment.

One by one he gave us our chance to escape by composing a rhyme. I did not understand at first, but as he went down the line demanding of each boy, "Make a good rhyme, and I shan't punish you," I caught the idea. When it was my turn I was ready for him, and answered promptly,

> "A szomszedom kopasz feju,
> Nem teremhet benne tetu."

> "My neighbor has a close-clipped head—
> There's no place there for a louse's bed."

A shout of laughter went up from the boys, for the lad next to me had his hair clipped to the roots and his head shone in the sunlit room like an ivory ball. Uncle Eszenyi himself laughed so heartily that there was nothing to do but release all the boys from punishment.

Our school was connected with the church, as are most schools in Hungary. Every Sunday we were compelled to attend the service, and the length and monotony of the sermon bored us beyond reason. From the gallery of the church hall a small door led to the bell tower from which could be seen the pattern of the town with its ancient moat and fortifications. It was a great temptation to sneak out during the sermon and go up there to enjoy the view. Naturally, this pleasure was forbidden. But I knew nothing of the rule, and during the first Sunday sermon, when one of my neighbors pointed to the little door and suggested the possibility of escape, I slipped quietly from my place and climbed to the tower where the

bells were hung. I was delighted with the green and vari-
colored roofs, cut into a giant jig-saw puzzle by the crooked
streets, and I failed to notice that Uncle Eszenyi could see me
from his garden, where he spent his Sunday mornings among
the beautiful beds. After the service he met us at the church
door, and pointing at me, he said severely, "You will report
your action tomorrow."

The rest of the class was amused at my predicament. It was
a favorite trick to send a new scholar to the tower, and the
boy who had got me into trouble was thumped on the back
and treated as a brilliant hero by the others.

I wandered about in misery until mealtime, fearful of what
awaited me next morning. Then just as Mother called us to
come in to dinner, I remembered Uncle Eszenyi's bargain the
day before. If I could make up another rhyme, he would not
punish me.

But the day was fine, and my younger brothers were eager
to explore the brick yard and the half-ruined factory, so I put
off rhyming till later on. We found heaped in one corner of
the yard a great quantity of unused brick, and scattered about
were many more. Gergely proposed that we build a house for
our old dog, Bodri. Our imaginations were carried away by
the idea, and such a building arose as might have fitted into an
old fairy tale—a palace with turrets and outworks—far too
fantastic for most dogs, but not for our Bodri. He had taught
all eight children to walk, and already little Janos, who was
just a year old, was clinging to the old dog's fur and toddling
about.

The afternoon was closing, but we still found time to make
a less elaborate home for our three little black pigs, and an-

other for our rabbits; some of those that had escaped into the night we had recaptured and brought home again, and we rewarded them with a magnificent hutch built entirely of brick.

So afternoon had slipped into evening, and it was supper-time and bedtime, and still I had no rhyme. I kept turning and rolling, wide awake and restless. My father finally could stand it no longer.

"What is the matter with you? Why don't you go to sleep?" he demanded from his own bed.

"Father, I am composing a rhyme, and I can't find the words," I answered.

"Are you crazy?" snorted my father. "I didn't move to the city for you to become a poet."

"No, Father," I explained. "I do not intend to be a poet, but I should like to save my skin tomorrow."

Father decided that I must have a fever, and called mother, who soon drew out of me the whole story, which satisfied them so that they both went quietly off to sleep. Not I. All night I pursued that rhyme.

In the class, those students who had the sad duty to "report" sat in a special place reserved near the master's desk. When I arrived I found two of my classmates already there, looking glum.

Uncle Eszenyi seemed to be in high spirits. "Well," he cried, "we have three nice plump pigeons here. We shall either hear their rhymes, or enjoy their songs."

The first student had no rhyme, but he gave the ingenious excuse that he had made one but lost it the moment he entered the classroom. Uncle Eszenyi turned to the class and asked solemnly whether anyone had found a rhyme. A wave of laughter ran over the room. The next boy had a rhyme, but it was a poor one, half stolen, so he too lost, by the decision of the class, which was always allowed to vote on the worth of the rhymes.

Now it was my turn. Worn out by the sleeplessness of the past night, I felt a bit dizzy as I rose to my feet. But I summoned all my strength and courage, and in a small voice I piped out:

> "Ahol nincs ott ne keress,
> Eszi bacsi szekeres."

> "Where there's nothing hidden away
> Do not search, little wagoner, pray."

Now, as you remember, Eszi means big eater, and that was the name we called Uncle Eszi which we thought he knew nothing about. My rhyme called forth a shout of laughter, and Uncle Eszenyi, who had not heard it distinctly, kept saying, "What? What? What did you say? Write it on the blackboard."

When the two lines were written on the board the class grew very still. Uncle Eszenyi stood a long, long time before the board. At last he turned. "Sandor, you have done well. That is not only a good rhyme, but it has a subtle meaning, it has reason, and above all, humor, which is the essence of a good couplet. You have, however, made fun of your old teacher, which is unpardonable in a grown boy, but since you came from the Puszta only a few days ago, I will excuse you. You seem clever," he added, "and strong enough to do more than the regular work. I shall make you monitor of the class, and right-hand boy in my office."

Admiring eyes followed me as I went to my place. As for Uncle Eszenyi, he looked back at the words written on the board, dreamily. I believe he was pleased with my reference to his famous song of "The Little Wagoner," and as he gazed at the poor little couplet he was thinking of the past, in the manner of old men.

SKIRMISHES
IN INFERNO STREET

Chapter Three

FOR A HUNDRED and fifty years Nagyvarad had been occupied by the Turks, who ruined the city's beautiful architecture completely. After the Asiatic custom they built their houses without any entrance toward the street; and with regard only to the probability of frequent battles, they made the streets zigzag fashion, with sharp corners every few feet.

This suited the purposes of the Turks, but it caused infinite trouble to the Hungarian inhabitants who regained possession of the city when the Turks were driven from Hungary and from Transylvania in the eighteenth century. It was exactly one hundred and fifty years after the Turks had left Nagy-varad that the Finta family arrived there, but a century and a half had not given the Hungarians time enough to raze and rebuild all the construction which had served as war barri-cades under the Turkish rule.

So, when we moved to Nagyvarad in 1892, we found it full of trouble which our enemies had prepared for us. We lived in that section where the most visible marks of the Turkish occupation still remained, where the streets were awkward for traffic, and dangerous. They were so narrow that a large cart was enough to block the whole street; they had no pavement, and were lighted by poor petroleum lamps. If a vehicle wanted to pass us, we had to stop and stand back to the wall.

Among these streets, the most dangerous and the most fa-mous was Inferno Street, through which we had to pass on our way to school. If some disaster occurred the first question asked would be, "Did it happen in Inferno Street?" If a man wanted his enemy to know that he was not afraid to face him, he would say, "I would like to meet you in Inferno Street!" Many duels were fought in that narrow passage and it was said that no man knew when he entered one end of the street whether he would live to leave the other.

The street was dark, with sharp corners every twenty-five or thirty feet. The paving was in terrible condition. Little win-dows faced the roadway, and gossips lingered in them to hear the remarks of those passing by, for conversations could be heard though the talkers were unseen. One had to be careful of the sharp corners if he wished to go unbruised, and not to collide with another person going in the opposite direction.

Such was Inferno Street. It was our fate to be set down at one end of it and be forced to go to school by it. During the first weeks when we had just learned how to get about, we met in this narrow way half a dozen other school boys. They belonged to another school, the rival of ours, as we learned later.

Without question or reason they began to attack us. Unfortunately we five brothers were soon divided by the sharp corners of the street wall. Besides, our attackers had all the advantages of boys brought up in the neighborhood. We took a terrible pounding, for there was no chance of escape. The only side street was blocked by the Koros River, which divided the city in two. Our one hope was to run away, but running in this narrow place held other dangers. Our attackers merely hooted at us, urging us to greater speed by making horrible noises behind us. At each corner they would arrive just in time to see us crash into the opposite wall, the way was so narrow, the corners so sharp, and our confusion so great.

The end of the street seemed an impossible distance away, and we reached it bruised and covered with inglorious dust, firmly resolved to avoid this street of horrors even if it meant a long detour to school. Better to be late and face the sharp tongue of Uncle Eszenyi.

But we forgot that by taking the longer route we would be just as late getting home. After several nights Father's suspicions were aroused. We had been late each night, with feeble excuses, and the smaller boys arrived home alarmingly weary, for the walk by the long way was over three miles. One morning Father decided to follow us, and that night he met us in the doorway.

"Why do you walk three miles to school when the little

walk down Inferno Street is nothing at all?"

Then I had to tell him. "Those Inferno Street boys are such fighters. They know tricks we have never learned. They gave such a beating . . ."

"You are cowards," was his short reply, and he turned on his heel and left us.

Then Saturday came, and Father made up for his cruel words by teaching us to fight. He showed us how to carve a blackjack, which we called a "hambone." It was to be fixed to the wrist by a strong soft skin in such a way that it could not be jerked off. Then he taught us how to form a triangle that could not easily be broken, and in this fighting formation on Monday morning we headed toward Inferno Street.

As we advanced, we each remembered what Father had said, that if we were beaten again he would force us to travel through this street every day until we learned to defend ourselves.

It was not long before we came upon our enemies, who were also on their way to school. They had not expected us to face them so soon again, and they fell upon us with a shout of laughter. The biggest one called, "What do you mean, pushing your way through here again!"

I did not answer him, but called over my shoulder to my brothers, "Draw the triangle tighter!" They moved forward with perfect precision.

For a moment the opponents, who today far outnumbered us, stood still with surprise. I shouted, "Now!" to my brothers, and the attack was on. About their shoulders fell our hambones in such quick blows that they were soon confused.

They could not escape in any direction, for the moment

they attempted it I gave the order to form our triangle there
and block the narrow way. At last we knew we had won. "Let
them go," I called, and they stumbled out of sight, more
bruised and sore than we had been the week before.

For a long time the Finta boys had free passage through
Inferno Street. Meanwhile our fame spread through the streets

of Nagyvarad, not only upon our own bank of the Koros River, but upon the left bank as well, where the rival school was situated, and where our enemies belonged.

But success did not make us careless. We never went to or from school without our hambones, which had proved their usefulness.

THE GREAT SNOW

Chapter Four

THE YEAR we moved to Nagyvarad, winter came early. There was snow by the end of October, and toward the middle of November came the heaviest snowfall anyone could remember. We could not go to school because of the great drifts blocking the streets, and these drifts deepened daily as the snow continued to fall. Traffic was absolutely paralyzed, and the country was threatened with starvation.

Our father was without work. Every day he walked to the city where he stayed all day searching for a job, but it was always in vain. One morning, to our sorrow, he put our three little black pigs into a sack, and throwing it across his powerful shoulders, bore the squealing bundle through the snow, fighting his way every step. The money he received for the pigs was just enough to pay the landlord for our rent.

The next night we heard a great noise outside the window. Father tried to investigate, but he was unable to force open the door, and then the wind began to howl again so that we heard nothing more for the rest of the night. Early the next morning, when Father had forced the door and dug a tunnel into the yard, he went to the doghouse for Bodri. Almost at once he was back again. Wolves had killed our beloved companion. The terrific storm continuing for so many days had driven them from their lairs, and they had entered the outskirts of the town and devoured all the dogs they had come upon. All of us wept brokenheartedly for Bodri, our parents too, and little Janos joined his grief to ours even though he hardly understood what had happened.

The next night there was another storm, and in the morning Father brought in more bad news. Foxes had caught our pet rabbits, in spite of our precautions in strengthening their pens. We had no more tears, having shed them all for poor Bodri, but all of us were terribly downcast. The snow no longer fell, and once more Father set out for the city to see if he could find money for provisions. He had been gone only a short while when the sun blazed forth. We ran joyfully to the window, only to see a flock of birds—hawks, owls, and even an eagle, attacking our pigeons that had ventured forth into the sun. They drove them high into the air and then fell upon them one after another.

We begged Mother to let us go out, but she knew there was nothing we could do, and would not let us go into the wet snow and bitter air. Would any of our pets be left? We did not see how.

Later that evening, when Father had arrived without food or money, we told him the story of our pigeons. He sat silent, and then, very slowly, he quoted from the Bible the verses about Job, who, when he had lost all his flocks and herds, lost even his children. When he reached that part of the story, Father looked up into Mother's face, and was once more silent, letting his eyes rest upon her. They did not make us feel that they expected cruel fate to overtake their children too, but rather that as long as we were all together we had cause to be grateful and content. That night the whole family went to bed hungry, but Father made us listen to a long prayer for our safekeeping, and for joy upon the morrow.

He turned to Mother. "Now, no more crying. We are warm, and we haven't starved yet. Surely something will turn up tomorrow."

Mother came to tuck us into bed, and when she fixed my covers I felt a warm drop fall upon my face. I caught her hand and said, trying to joke as my father would have, "Well, Mother, after the big snow a little rain, eh?" But she covered my mouth with her trembling hand, lest Father hear me and seeing her weakness, lose courage.

Father left home so early the next day that we did not hear him go. When we woke, Mother had no breakfast to give us, but she tried to tell us funny stories. I was the oldest, and felt closest to my parents in their grief and need, and while I listened to her voice I turned to the window so that I should not have to watch her sad face. The windows were spread with exquisite frost flowers, delicate and lovely, but at the top the warmth of the room had melted them. Through this narrow strip I stared unseeing at the sky. Then, all at once, my eyes were caught by the flight of some birds.

Those many months on the Puszta as herdboy had made me a student of birds, and I knew at once that those flying past our windows were rare indeed. I had only half an ear now for my mother's tales. A plan came into my head. Those birds were as hungry as the owls and hawks of yesterday. Could I not set a snare for them?

I left the circle of my hungry brothers and sisters and slipped into the other room where stood our empty cages. Of one of them I made a trap such as I had used on the plains. I tiptoed to the door, and passed through the tunnel of snow. My pockets were stuffed with squash and sunflower seeds, and as soon as I was in the yard, I cleared away the snow from the top of poor Bodri's castle, set my trap there, and scattered a quantity of seeds upon its floor.

The birds were so ravenous that they could hardly wait until I had finished fixing the snare. The moment I stepped back they swooped down and in a few seconds the cage was filled with birds. And what birds! The finest and rarest I had ever seen fought for an entrance to my baited trap. It was only their hunger that made them so foolhardy. I knew I must not wait till all the seeds had been eaten, so I slipped up back of the door, and shut it fast. There was the cage, full of strange and beautiful birds, and so I carried it into the house where mother was still beguiling the others with her fairy tales.

When Istvan saw my cage he gave a yell. The others jumped

to their feet and crowded about me, and Mother, who no longer had an audience, joined them. At first they stood speechless as I held the cage high so each could see my beautiful prizes. Then they tried to identify each bird. They shouted to me to tell them what this one was called, and that one, and where they had come from, and how I had caught them.

"Bring all the old cages from the store room," I ordered Gergely and Istvan. "We'll mend them and fill them all."

I was a hero now even in the eyes of Rose and Marie, my sisters, and they obeyed me willingly. Mother lent a hand in the repairing of the cages, which had been half wrecked on that unlucky night of our arrival.

Soon we had housing room for all the birds I had caught. While the others mended more cages, I set my trap again, and yet again. Six times that day I took it out empty save for a few sunflower seeds, and brought it back filled with rare and lovely birds. It was growing dusk when I brought in the final snaring, and we had scarcely transferred the last to smaller cages when little Mateh shouted from the window, "Father! Here's Father!" To have everything in readiness for him, we dared not stop what we were doing, but it was hard to resist when Mateh added, "He has a big, big parcel." And he measured off a truly magnificent space in the air with his little arms.

"It must be food," sighed Mother. All at once we knew how hungry we were, for we had not had one mouthful all that day.

When Father entered the house, his face was lined with fatigue and concern, and with the greatest care he placed his heavy burden on the floor. We saw that he wore no overcoat, but had wrapped it about the bundle. Before he spoke he stood rubbing his arms for a moment, for they were stiff from cold. All he said was, "Sandor, bring a bowl of snow, at once."

While I obeyed, I heard Mother ask timidly, "Have you brought food?"

"No," replied Father, "but I have brought a boy—a frozen boy. I found no work again today, but as I returned homeward this evening I discovered this poor boy. He was lying on the bank of the river just outside the city, entirely covered with snow except for the tip of his cap. I am not sure we can revive him!"

"Alas," cried poor Mother, "no food, and more children!"

But she was not so unkind as her cry of dismay made her seem. With the greatest care she and Father unwrapped the frozen boy. For nearly two hours they took turns rubbing him with handfuls of snow which we brought them in a bowl. He seemed not to breathe, but at last there was a long sighing sound, and we knew he was alive. After that he recovered rapidly, and soon opened his eyes and spoke in a feeble whisper. But he stared straight before him, so we knew he was in delirium.

Father told Rose and Marie to make a bed for him, and the bottle of milk which was all Father had brought from the city and which he had meant for our baby, was fed to the unconscious boy. It took a long time, and great patience, to spoon the milk between his lips, but Father did not stop until all the milk had been swallowed.

The other children were so exhausted by the hunger and excitement of the long day that one by one they had now gone off to their beds till only Mother and Father and I were left. Father dropped into his chair and lit his pipe, and his sad eyes seemed to say, "This is life, my boy. One goes out to get work and food and money for his family. Instead he finds a child lost in the snow for whom nobody cares."

He looked so discouraged that I longed to comfort him. I did not know how to begin to tell him of our day's adventure, so I went into the store room and brought back a cage full of birds. He seemed to waken from a dream, smiled, and pointing at each bird in turn, gave them all their proper names. Eagerly I listened, for some of the names I had never heard before.

All at once, he sat up straight. "Those birds!" he said, "They're rare enough to be valuable. Why, I can surely get twenty-five pengoes (about ten dollars) for them in the city. Who caught them?"

Proudly I answered, "I did, sir. And this is not the only

cage. There are many more in the store room."

That night there was no sleep for me. With Mother's help, Father and I made many small cages. Carefully we classified each bird, and before the younger children were awake, Father had left, carrying the cages off with him.

As soon as the others awoke Mother began telling them about the boy who was ill, and how quiet they must be, how helpful to her while she was nursing him. She told them that if he lived he was to be our new brother. Each child had a turn to watch by the bedside.

At noon, Father returned with another heavy and extremely precious cargo. His face was wreathed in smiles, and we all gathered round—even Istvan, whose turn it was to watch beside the sleeping boy—waiting to see what was in the bundle. Like a real Santa Claus, Father had brought the favorite food of every member of the family. One by one, with a little joke, he pointed out each parcel. Mother began at once to stir the fire in the stove, and soon the smell of cooking, the sweetest smell that can reach the noses of those who have tightened their belts for many days past, filled our sunny kitchen.

While we were opening the bundles, Father went to the side of the cot. And so it happened that after all it was he who saw the sick boy's eyes open. He spoke in a low voice, and his own eyes were tender. "The boy is awake." When we would have rushed to crowd about the sickbed, he shook his head at us. Then he turned back and began to talk in a gentle tone. The lad, who might have been ten or eleven, answered in a weak voice. "My name is Lucas." If he had any other name, he did not know it.

Among ourselves, while Father talked to the boy, we de-

cided on a second name, "Fagyos," which in English means
"icy." Mother poured some broth from the stew she was making, and when the boy had drunk he fell again into a quiet
sleep.

After dinner, which was a real celebration, Father went back
to watch over his new-found son, and we boys decided once
more to try our luck at catching birds. We were almost as
successful as we had been the day before. Gergely and Istvan,
and even Arpad, who was just eight, were good carpenters,
and they made more cages.

During the next few weeks, we succeeded so well with
our birds that we soon had money and food for several months
to come. The light came back into our parents' faces, the
spring into their step. The night when Lucas was strong
enough to sit up, Father said, "Let's have a party!" He told
stories, and made up ridiculous games, and kept us laughing
all the evening long. At the end, when he saw Lucas was growing tired, he said, "We are moving tomorrow to the city. We
didn't come here to catch birds, nor to make money, but to
educate you boys. That means you, too, Lucas," he said to the
boy propped up in his chair with great pillows. "You are one
of my sons."

When Lucas, who had never known either his father or his
mother, heard that, his sad face took on a broad smile which
he wore ever afterward. He never laughed much, but his
smile was as broad as the moon in its first quarter, and because
he was so jolly and because his coming had changed the fortunes of the family, he soon became the pet of everybody,
from baby Janos to Rose, who was fifteen and quite grown up.
He recovered his health rapidly, but his terrible experience in

the snow storm left him half deaf. This sometimes caused funny situations when he tried to join in the conversation, and we laughed at him, but he never lost his good nature or his wide smile.

THE BEST WAY TO SING

Chapter Five

THE NEXT day Father went to look for apartments in town. When he had found one which suited him, he hired a wagoner to come and move our things next day, and then he hurried home to tell us. All that day we packed, and we were ready for the wagoner when he came. Lucas had the easiest part, for he was still too weak to walk. Father wrapped him in a heavy blanket and carried him on his shoulder. We thought it tremendously exciting to change homes, and we bounded beside the cart with whoops and catcalls. A drift across the way presented no difficulty to such husky boys. When the cart stuck, we dug it out again. We rather hoped to meet our old enemies of Inferno Street and show off our prowess before Father and Lucas. Luckily for the windows in the neighborhood, they did not appear. But on the morrow we would start to school again, and we talked of that, as we plodded through the drifts, and of the time when Lucas could go too.

On the way Father told us how he had come to rent the apartment. The landlord was a bachelor and did not live in the building, so Father had hoped he would not mind a large family. Just the same, the landlord asked Father if he had any children.

"Yes, I have," he replied. "We even have an orphan boy, who has been lying in bed for a long time."

The landlord thought he meant he had only the one child, and asked nothing further about the family. He signed the agreement, and so the place was ours.

We boys were interested especially in the woodhouse and the large porch which extended from the kitchen into the back yard. That woodhouse could be used not only for storing fuel but also as a workroom. All of us were born with an itch to carve. When we were young it was wood, and as we grew older we tried our tools on any material—iron, clay, bronze, or stone. So we begged permission to set up a woodcarving studio. Permission was given for that, and also, but with more difficulty, for keeping our pets on the back porch. We installed them with great delight, though not without quarreling about which space belonged to whom. Father finally settled the dispute by stretching strings from floor to ceiling, thus measuring off areas for each of us.

The next day we returned to school. On our arrival Uncle Eszenyi demanded to know where we had been these past two weeks, and I told him the story of how we had been blockaded by the storm, how the wolves and foxes had devoured our pets, and last, the capture of the birds, and the finding of Lucas. It was a dramatic and interesting tale, and it strengthened my standing with Uncle Eszenyi. I was going to need that standing sooner than I expected.

They teach the children singing in every school in Hungary, but in our school it had become the most important subject. Every day at the opening and closing of the classes we sang, and in the afternoon, the last hour was devoted to singing instruction.

Uncle Eszenyi often told us that we made him the saddest

man in the world because we were worthless when it came to singing. We had poor voices, and no feeling, he said.

Day after day we heard the same criticism, and one day he just gave up and left us in the middle of the singing lesson. As he went out the door, he asked me to take charge of the class and teach them the words and music of the songs, which I had managed to learn fairly well. From that afternoon I became the substitute singing teacher. At first, I confess, I had little better success than Uncle Eszenyi, but that was before I discovered the secret of singing.

As monitor of the class, I had charge of heating the room, and it was also my duty each day to go to the cellar for Uncle Eszenyi's supply of wine.

The people of Hungary are like many others; most of them drink moderately, some drink to excess, and there are some who live a lifetime without finding their limit. Uncle Eszenyi was certain that he knew his own limit, and each fall, he arranged with the wine merchant to deliver the amount which by his calculation would last him until the next fall.

Each day I would fill his "oros," or pitcher. It held a gallon of wine, and had to be handled with the greatest care and respect, for it had been used by three generations.

I had noticed that when Uncle Eszenyi was about to give us a lesson in singing he first paid an extra long visit to the oros. It stood in a high closet in the classroom, the door of which, when it was open, hid him from view.

As Uncle Eszenyi's birthday drew near, we wanted to learn a new song to surprise him. I was ashamed of the class because they could not learn the music, and one day I decided to try a scheme. Just before the singing lesson, while Uncle Eszenyi was away from the room, I went down to the cellar and brought up a generous supply of wine which I poured into the tank that held our drinking water. Uncle Eszenyi used to say, when we failed to reach the high notes of the music, that our voices were rusty. The wine wrought an instant miracle. The boys' voices were like the voices of flutes, and they were able to learn the song with scarcely any effort.

For three days I repeated my scheme, and then came the great event—Uncle Eszenyi's birthday celebration. Before the usual singing lesson period, I made a speech, and I told him how greatly we appreciated his good will toward us. I called upon the stars in the sky to be witness of the strength of our affection for him, which was the best gift we could make in return for what he had taught us. Finally, I wished him, according to the Hungarian custom, "wine from Tokay, wheat from the Hungarian plain, and good will from every man's heart."

After my speech, I asked permission for the class to sing a new song which we had learned especially for his birthday. Uncle Eszenyi had listened to the speech and it seemed to please him, but when I spoke of the song, he lost patience.

"You need not sing it. I will appreciate it more if it is left unsung. Do you want to spoil my birthday mood?"

But I begged and insisted, and the other boys added their pleas. He agreed at last, but as we began our performance, he seemed to pay not the slightest attention, but stared deliberately out of the window.

We had been prudent enough to take our drink of wine, the "oil" for rusty voices, before the birthday ceremonies began; at my signal the boys now stood and began to sing.

Pretty soon Uncle Eszenyi's gaze left the window, and was turned upon us in wonder. My baton moved in steady rhythm, and the boys' voices followed it in silver tones, like an organ. His expression of wonder deepened as we sang on and on. His small eyes watched us, fixed and wide, and his mouth, surrounded by the reddest mustache in Hungary, dropped open.

He could stand it no longer. Abruptly he motioned me to my place and led the rest of the birthday song himself, with the greatest pleasure beating time and nodding his head. At the end of that song, we sang his own best and most famous, *The Little Wagoner*, and still he did not recover from his astonishment. How had we suddenly developed this ability to sing?

But we did not tell. Our secret, for the time, remained a secret. We left school that afternoon well pleased with ourselves. Shouting to one another, we started home. The temperature had risen during the day, and the snow had begun to melt. Almost immediately the city's streets turned to mud, and we walked into more mud at every corner.

We tried to avoid the deepest puddles, jumping from one solid spot of ground to another, but we had no sooner turned into the narrow way of Inferno Street than we had to run recklessly, for we were attacked on every side by boys from the school on the left bank of the Koros River. We were wholly unprepared, because we had passed undisturbed along this way for several weeks now. The enemy crowded after us, and we headed for the other end of the street in a mad rush. But they had laid a trap for us, and in a trice we were *running the gauntlet*.

This pleasant sport needs two groups of boys. The leaders of the other school had divided their forces; one group was waiting silently down the street ahead of us, the other was attacking us from behind. The moment the first group heard the shouts of their companions, they began to run down the street, just ahead of us. But they paused long enough before each house to ring its bell, or beat upon the door, not once, but eight or ten times. The furious inhabitants rushed into the street with brooms and brushes, mops and walking sticks; in short, whatever came handiest and would be useful for beating bad boys. And we were the boys who arrived just in time to receive the beatings!

At the end of our dash, we were a sight to behold. Among us we had a splendid collection of black eyes, and we were splattered with mud and aching in every bone.

MOUSE IN? MOUSE OUT?

Chapter Six

EACH MORNING as we started off for school, I remembered with shame that we had never repaid our enemies for making us run the gauntlet. Planning revenge for that painful experience I took upon myself, as leader.

At last I thought of a plan. I would form a new boys' club, and with our army thus increased, we would plan a counter attack that would be bound to succeed. My brothers agreed, so one bright spring day we started forth. Each of us carried on his shoulders a cage containing one of our most beautiful birds, and we went parading up and down the street. Lucas, who was now well enough to join us, carried a large painted sign which informed onlookers that

IN OUR CLUB

THERE ARE MANY BRAVE PRIVATES

CLEVER COMMANDERS AND OFFICERS

ARE WANTED

Our little birds dancing and chirping in their clean cages in the bright sunshine attracted a crowd of boys, but when we tried to register them in our club, that was another matter. Meanwhile, our enemies, holding a large placard, were marching from the opposite direction. As they neared us we read:

MARCH UPON THE BRAVE

AND

FALL INTO YOUR GRAVE!

Fearing trouble, the boys who had gathered about us immediately crowded into our courtyard. It was not courage that brought them, but there were a lot of them, and we took immediate advantage of the situation. Istvan shouted, "All those in the courtyard are fully registered members of our

Club, or else get off our property." They thought it too risky
to leave, under the circumstances, so they joined us then and
there.

The next day I proposed a way of repaying the rival boys,
and asked for volunteers from our Club. Lucas was eager to
share in our fortunes, good or bad, so I gave him an important
role in the advance troop. We waited at the head of the street,
each boy in his place. Everything was going as I had planned,
and our enemies had just entered the mouth of Inferno Street,
when Lucas, because of his bad hearing which made him mis-
understand my instructions, caught sight of the boys and gave
his alarm cry too early. They began at once to retreat, pre-
ferring a battle with our main force at the mouth of the way
to running the gauntlet the way they had made us run it. We
tried to force them back, using our hambones freely, but in
the confusion that followed our army vanished like thin air,
and only Istvan and I were left fighting side by side. Our fight
ended as abruptly and unfortunately as it began. A heavy hand
fell upon my shoulder, and I turned to look directly into the
face of the principal of the other school. His boys cheered
for "Uncle Ratkay," as they called him, for he took from us
our war clubs—the hambones—and after boxing our jaws he
sent us home.

The next day Uncle Eszenyi sent me and my brother Istvan,
who was our best fighter, to the other school to apologize to
the principal, and take our punishment, whatever it might be.
Uncle Ratkay was a humorist. He was a writer, and edited and
published the only humorous journal in Nagyvarad. We
knew, therefore, that he would find a very special and original
punishment for us, and were not mistaken.

I was made to wear two pieces of one of the hambones suspended from my ears, and Istvan had to carry his in his mouth, like a dog, and thus we had to go into every class in the school and show ourselves. It was a bitter lesson, and for a long time after we tried to avoid all fights.

Uncle Eszenyi soon forgave us this escapade, because he was so proud of our improvement in singing. Then, near the end of the school year, I returned from the cellar one day with Uncle Eszenyi's oros absolutely empty. When I reported to him that there was no more wine in the large barrel he looked at me as if I had lost my mind.

"What did you say? No wine in the big barrel? That is impossible! Never before in all my life has my wine given out at this time of year." He stuttered excitedly. "Come with me," he said. "I want to see for myself."

The class knew only too well where Uncle Eszenyi's wine had gone. We had had the last of it that very day before our singing lesson.

Uncle Eszenyi made his way painfully down into the cellar with me, and there he had to face the dreadful truth, that the wine barrel was indeed empty. He examined it on all sides, and the tap, and the cellar floor all about it, but no leak could he find. Then he shook his head sadly, and said with a perplexed sigh:

"Well, such a thing has never happened before—never. No empty wine barrel ever had a place in my cellar."

He pointed out another, a much smaller barrel, and told me that thereafter I was to draw the wine from that one.

During the following week I had no chance to feed my songsters with wine, and besides, the fact that the big barrel had been emptied made me uneasy. The boys now became the most incorrigible lazy-bones in all Hungary. They just stopped singing; their voices no longer had any volume or sweetness, and so they gave up entirely.

Uncle Eszenyi noticed the change, and scolded about it. He was particularly upset on the last day of the week because the superintendent of the district was to visit our school. He had tried to teach us a new song for the occasion, and we had been progressing nicely when the wine barrel gave out. On that important morning Uncle Eszenyi faced us with sorrow on his lean face. "Boys," he said, "I am ashamed of myself that I have not been able to teach you that simple song. What can I say to our superintendent? What? What?"

We had few lessons that morning, for until the man arrived all Uncle Eszenyi could do was shake his head and gaze at us mournfully. A knock came at the door. He left us to go into the office with the superintendent, and at once I carried the water tank to the cellar and filled it from the small barrel. This was Uncle Eszenyi's oldest wine, and it was very strong. I let the class sip a drink apiece to warm them up a little.

We had hardly had time to finish when Uncle Eszenyi and the superintendent entered the classroom. We greeted them with an unusually hearty welcome, which must have puzzled our teacher. The superintendent examined the class, and at the end of the examination, he asked, because he thought Uncle Eszenyi would expect him to, for the new song.

Uncle Eszenyi, with apology in every tone, told the superintendent that he had had no opportunity to produce a new song that year. "That class," he said sadly, "has no feeling for the high art of music."

The superintendent thought that he only wanted more urging, and persisted, till finally there was nothing Uncle Eszenyi could do but give in. He eyed us reproachfully as he gave the name of a song that was annoyingly familiar to every ear in Nagyvarad. However, while he had been out of the room we had agreed that at his signal we should begin the song it had been his ambition to teach us for this day.

Poor Uncle Eszenyi almost went out of his senses as he heard the first strains of that difficult song. He made frantic gestures for us to stop, but we paid no attention to him, and as we reached note after note with accuracy, he stopped the windmill whirling of his arms. We really knew the song, and we gave our best to it.

When the superintendent left the room, after expressing himself as being more than satisfied with our class and its standing, Uncle Eszenyi praised our singing. Yet he was curious, we could see, to know the secret and source of this sudden skill.

Next morning, I felt uneasy in class. However, the morning passed in its regular routine, and our teacher did not refer to the miracle of the day before. Near the noon hour he called, as he had every day during the year, "Sandor, the oros."

As I rose and started out with the oros, he asked me to come to his desk. There he took a piece of white chalk in his hand and made a circle about my mouth.

As I went down cellar, I smiled, thinking, "Well, old man, you can't catch me that way. Today I shall not drink a drop of your precious wine."

But when I smelled the sweet bouquet I could not resist sipping a very small draught. Then, laughing, I took from my pocket a small piece of chalk and carefully traced a white ring around my mouth just as Uncle Eszenyi had done. Calmly and quietly I went back to the classroom carrying the heavy oros brimming over with the best wine of the Ermellek.

As I entered the door with my precious cargo and my white-ringed mouth, the whole class burst into a laugh. Uncle Eszenyi first took the oros, then he turned me about and showed me to the class, pointing at my mouth.

"You, sir," he said, "are the guilty one who has been drinking my wine. You thought I marked your mouth with chalk. I had a piece of chalk in my hand, but it was only my finger that marked an imaginary circle about your lips."

Never before had I felt so humiliated. If there had only been a mirror—but then, in that dark cellar I should not have seen myself anyway. And so he had tricked me, and I had come back to the classroom looking like a clown. If I had only resisted my thirst!

To Uncle Eszenyi, this was sure evidence of how all his wine had disappeared. He revoked his trust in me, and I was no longer right-hand boy, nor monitor of the class. I went home that night the sorriest lad in Nagyvarad. When I looked about me for sympathy, I found none, and I grew more and more hurt, for it seemed to me my classmates had no business being in such high good humor over my tragedy, or that they at least might take the pains to hide their amusement. Day after day they joked and teased me, until I was determined to get even.

One afternoon, just before the time that Uncle Eszenyi generally entered, I noticed in the drawer of my desk a small dead mouse. I did not know what a bad humor I was in. I caught it and held it high, saying, "See what I have found!"

The class paid no attention, but went on laughing and joking. I was spoiled by the long time when they had had to listen to me because I was monitor, and now I grew more and more indignant. "Well," I said, "I'll give you something to laugh at." I ran to the closet in which Uncle Eszenyi's oros was hidden, and disappeared behind the door.

I had hardly returned to my seat when Uncle Eszenyi came back into the room. None of the boys, not even the new monitor, had the courage to tell him. In fact, they were not sure whether I had really dropped the mouse into the oros, for I had been hidden behind the door. All afternoon they waited for that moment when our old teacher would lift high the base of the ancient pitcher. Every student was occupied with the most interesting question of that whole school year: "Mouse in or mouse out?"

When Uncle Eszenyi finally opened the closet door, every gaze was glued upon that narrow panel which shut the figure of the old man from view. It was a most dramatic moment, and I, having brought it about, felt much better about my reputation with my classmates.

Uncle Eszenyi picked up the oros with his accustomed nonchalance, shook it a little, lifted it, and slowly sipped. We counted the swallows; seven long pulls we counted before he stopped. But he was only resting, and added another long draught. Then he closed the door of the closet and with his large square red handkerchief wiped away half a dozen unnaturally large tears from his eyes. He observed, more to himself than to the class, "*Some* grape juice!" That was all. "*Some* grape juice!"

We all sat immobile. No one had the courage to move so much as a little finger for fear that if he did he would burst into uncontrollable laughter, and the rest with him. It was as if we were frozen into our seats. The lesson could make no progress—Uncle Eszenyi could get no replies from any of us. At length, exasperated, he turned to me.

"Sandor, I am going to put you in charge of the class again. Since you stopped being monitor they act as if they had lost their senses. Nothing ever happens here any more—not even any fun!" And he went out of the room.

We waited until we were positive that he was out of earshot, and then the room rocked with mirth—such laughter as

the old place had probably never heard though three generations of boys had passed through it. As soon as we would get
quieted down from exhaustion, the laughter would start
afresh as someone mimicked the old man, "Nothing ever
happens here—*not even any fun!*" The ceiling almost burst.

WE BUY
A LITTLE EUM

Chapter Seven

AT THE END of Inferno Street
stood a stationer's shop. The owner, Mr.
Haldeck, had migrated from Galicia to Nagyvarad. He complained once to my father of his unfortunate situation in that
infamous little thoroughfare, and Father asked him how it

happened that he had chosen it for his place of business. "Why," said Father, "it's the battlefield of all the school children of Nagyvarad."

Mr. Haldeck replied with resignation. "Well, Mr. Finta, it was chiefly on account of the children that I chose it. When I first came from Galicia I went about looking for a street where lots of children came and went, and I had never seen so many of them in so small a space as I counted in Inferno Street. I made a dreadful mistake. No child has money to spend if he comes from a family where there are as many as six children. And around Inferno Street no family exists which has less than six."

Children are the best and also the worst customers of a stationer's shop. If a child has money, he is ready to spend it at once, and without reserve; but give him a chance to choose among two hundred objects in a stationery shop, and be sure that he will want the two hundred and first piece which is not even in the shop, but which he expects to be shown next!

When we had the good fortune to possess a penny we went to Mr. Haldeck's to spend it. He always grew nervous when he saw us coming. Since his was the only shop in the neighborhood which sold toys and novelties from Nuremberg or Vienna, it was the place we always chose. We never went alone; we took not only all the children of our family, but we called in our friends as well. Poor old Mr. Haldeck had good reason to stroke his long beard when our gang appeared in his shop.

"Do not touch anything here," he would tell us the moment we entered. "Everything is to be looked at. Nothing is to be handled. How much money have you in all?" He was cautious regarding money, because usually eight or ten children went to buy two cents' worth, and spent half an hour choosing it. We would first inquire the price of the toy locomotives or steam-run toys, and gradually came down to the usual six marbles only after we had exhausted the information about all the larger things in the shop.

The upper portion of Mr. Haldeck's shop door was of glass, divided into nine small panes. Upon these were painted the names of the different types of merchandise he carried in stock. On the last three had been the word

PE TROL EUM

but his careless customers, on coming in and out, had broken the first two panes. When he had replaced them, he had neglected to repaint the letters, so that all that was left of the word was EUM.

One day I had an idea. Carrying a small bottle I entered Mr. Haldeck's shop and asked him for two cents' worth of "eum." At first Mr. Haldeck did not understand what I said, but he did not like to admit it; after a long pause in which he stroked his beard he asked me to repeat my order. I jerked my thumb at the small window-pane where the syllable "eum" still remained. My face was perfectly straight, so at first Mr. Haldeck smilingly nodded his head. Then, suddenly realizing I was poking fun at him, he gave me an unfriendly shove through the door of his shop, saying, "Boy! Boy! Boy!"

Half an hour later I sent one of my brothers, Gergely, to Mr. Haldeck for "eum." He came out of the shop so quickly he was almost flying. In another half hour our third brother,

Istvan, went in and came out as quickly. In the next few days, all our friends who were bold enough to ask for "eum" had a friendly meeting with Mr. Haldeck.

From then on, if the shopkeeper saw a group of us gathering near his door, he would take his hardwood yardstick and like a soldier with sword in hand stand waiting for any boy who would have nerve enough to ask for "eum."

Among the schoolboys from the other side of the river was a big, bad-tempered and very strong boy named John Chiken; we called him Chik. He was the bully of the entire neighborhood. It was sad indeed for the small boy who came in sight of Chik when he was in a bad temper. And he was in a bad temper almost every day, for he was constantly failing in his recitations at school, and he had not been promoted for several years.

When Chik appeared on the playground, the little boys at once stopped their games, whatever they were, and went elsewhere.

On the last day of school, after we had received our certificates, we were engrossed in each other as we paraded along in fine spirits, chatting over the good grades we had earned. Then Lucas, like a bad conscience, whispered that Chik was standing in the middle of the narrow way. We could see that he was in a terrible temper, and we surmised that he had failed again. It was a most unfortunate meeting, for Chik was certain to want to make someone pay for his humiliation. Taken thus by surprise, we had no chance of escape. We moved forward in apprehension, and Chik, likewise silent, fell in with us as we approached him, and stalked along beside us.

As we neared the shop of Mr. Haldeck, Lucas was seized

with a wild idea. With his face as innocent as a baby's, he turned to Chik and asked him whether he had been to Haldeck's to ask for "eum." "Because," said Lucas, "we have all been to Haldeck's for 'eum', and if you are as nervy as you pretend to be, and not just a coward, here's the chance to prove it. Let's see you go in and buy some 'eum.'"

Lucas's suggestion was as dangerous as a match thrown into a powder barrel.

"How do I ask for 'eum'?" Chik demanded, not wanting to show that he didn't know what it was.

Lucas produced a small bottle from his pocket and explained the procedure.

With great arrogance, Chik announced, "I'll bring some. And if one of you moves while I'm gone. . . ."

I called after him in as friendly a voice as I could muster, "Ask for two cents' worth, and be sure it's the best."

He grunted, and carrying the little bottle, left us swinging his shoulders in his most belligerent manner. When he had disappeared inside Mr. Haldeck's shop we drew close together and waited.

All at once the cries of Chik rent the air! Mr. Haldeck was evidently in a bad mood that day—or else he had decided to put a stop once and for all to small boys annoying him. At any rate, he had decided to give the next "eum" buyer such a lesson that none of us would bother him again.

When at last Chik came tumbling out of the door of the shop he was howling. Lucas went up to him and to the astonishment of all of us, asked, "Well, didn't you bring the 'eum'?" Chik was more humiliated by Lucas's taunt than by the beating Mr. Haldeck had given him. Although by this time there was a great audience of small boys gathered around him, he could not stop crying, and this public shame ended forever his career as the bully of Inferno Street.

FIRST
GLIMPSES OF SCIENCE

Chapter Eight

MY FATHER, who was a born artist, writer, talker, wood-carver, engineer, and a man skilled in the handling of horses, was also a humorist and a wise teacher. He had many devices for calling to our attention something he thought we should learn, and he was able to interest us in anything he thought would be to our benefit, or would advance our knowledge of the sciences.

Shortly after we had moved from the old brick factory into the heart of the city, he took a job as engineer in a big wood-impregnating factory where we visited him regularly, carrying his meals to him twice a day. We enjoyed this errand, for it gave us a chance to watch the big machines. Father was never too busy to explain them to us, and he would go into great detail. Never less than three boys carried his lunch to him, and long before school closed we had become deeply interested in the study of mechanics. When vacation came Father took us to the public library and taught us how to use the library, and what sort of books to choose.

My first book dealt with aeronautics, and I was particularly fascinated by the descriptions of ballooning. I read the story of the Mongolfier brothers, who succeeded in making the first balloon ascension. When I had finished reading about those air adventurers and their contribution to the art of flying, I was eager to add my own bit to the science.

Our woodshed, which had become the clubhouse for the boys on our side of the river, became a very popular place as soon as we announced our intention of conquering the air. My brother Gergely, who had turned to electricity, declared that he had set out to make thunder the obedient servant of man. To outdo Gergely I wrote a notice upon a wooden board to the effect that in one more week I should be ready to take every member of the Club into the air. Immediately the attendance at our meetings doubled, which meant a fat treasury, for each member paid two cents into our common bank. We hung a sign on the wall of the woodshed:

ONE MORE WEEK AND WE SHALL FLY

This angered the other club, composed of boys from the

school across the river, and they set up a large wooden board
and printed across it:

ONE MORE WEEK

AND WE SHALL SEE

WHAT A BIG BUM

THE OLDEST FINTA BOY IS

They took their sign and paraded through all the streets,
and even had the nerve to pass our door.

My first trick was to be a parachute jump. I chose the parachute because I thought it would be a trick easy to perform
with people in the street, and it did not require a great capital
investment. I expected to be spectacular.

The more I thought over my plans, the more elaborate they
became. My parachute must travel not only vertically, but
horizontally, and as rapidly both ways as possible. I wished
not only to make a high jump, but a long one, and my ambition was to cross the Koros River. Each day now as I passed
the river which flowed in such profound calm I thought to
myself, "It hasn't the slightest idea that I intend to make it
famous."

I decided that an umbrella would serve me in my parachute jump, if only it were well constructed. The deeper I
delved into the study of aeronautics, the stronger grew my
temptation to test the endurance of my mother's good umbrella. It was a large sized one, made of shiny silk, used only
on holidays, or when Mother made her occasional short visits
to our relatives.

One day, under pretext of wishing to clean the silver handle for her, I asked for the umbrella.

Mother was surprised and suspicious. "Sandor," she said, "you have something on your mind." She knew too well that when we offered our services voluntarily we had some hidden motive. As soon as I had gone away without the umbrella she hid it from me.

To accomplish my feat, which was to be performed the next Sunday, was no longer a question of honor for me personally, but involved the honor of our whole Club. Each day, the first thing in the morning, I went to the Koros River to study the currents, both air and water. The water in the river bed was narrow because of the summer drought, but it was deep, so that there was a good chance of drowning if my calculation for the high and wide jump should not work out well. These problems always occupy the inventor's mind. On further consideration, I decided it would be wise to make some other experiment first, choosing solid ground rather than the river bed.

It was a great thrill when I finally discovered my mother's umbrella where she had hidden it. Five minutes after, I was on the roof of our shed, and before Mother could see and stop me, I had the umbrella wide and was performing the trick which is the very A B C of aeronautics. I flung myself boldly into the air. What happened next takes no time at all to tell. I came down to earth at once, as I had expected, but the umbrella was inside out, which I had not expected. The treachery of that shining umbrella was a considerable mystery to me. I did not know why it had failed me, but I did know that I ached. Luckily, no member of the Club had witnessed my accident. Only my mother's transformed umbrella lay beside me as a witness of my first disaster. I concluded that I must certainly find some place other than the river for my public performance, and that another and better-built umbrella must be my equipment.

The fall had robbed me of my gaiety and I sat quietly in a corner of the room. Mother noticed that, and said uneasily, "Sandor, you are too good today." But before she could ask any questions, Father came home, and as always when he had something interesting to tell, he shouted, "Good news!"

We crowded about him, and he told us that he had just heard that someone had discovered the ancient walls of the cathedral in which the ashes of St. Ladislau had been buried on July 29th, 1095. St. Ladislau was the most famous of the legendary kings of Hungary, and it was he (so they said), who had founded Nagyvarad. The legend told how the idea for founding the city was suggested to him by an angel whom he met in the woods while he was hunting with a band of courtiers. There were many stories about him; he was leader, appointed by the Pope, of the united army of the crusaders of Europe, but he died before he could start for the Holy Land. His ashes were buried under the shrine of the cathedral in the city he had built. During many centuries, the burial place had been a sacred spot where miracles were performed. Sometimes, in famous trials, witnesses had been brought before the grave of St. Ladislau and there proved their truthfulness. It was believed that those who were innocent would not be burned when they thrust their hands into a flame which burned always before the shrine.

During the invasion of the Turks, and their occupation, the

city was so altered in appearance that after their expulsion no one could find even the foundation stones of that famous cathedral where the sacred ashes of St. Ladislau were resting.

The evening when my first attempt at flying had ended so badly, the discovery of the site of that long-lost cathedral was the most talked of subject in the city. The site lay under the fortress which had been rebuilt many times, first by the Turks, and later by the Hungarians when they regained and struggled to keep the city.

My brothers and sisters and I listened to Father's story of St. Ladislau, and we kept him until bedtime recalling legends, and the few historical facts. He sent us to bed with the promise that the next day, his free day from the factory, we should all go to see the fortress. We agreed that Father was the best in the world.

The old fortress of Nagyvarad, which is used even today as an armory, was constructed of stone and brick, with massive walls. It was built in the bed of the Koros River in such a way that the river formed a moat about the fortress in the old days. Today that part of the river bed is dry, and the deep trench is used by the soldiers as a drilling ground; the channel of the river has been deflected and the water flows past the fortress in a well-built stone bed.

The next afternoon when we arrived at the fortress, we found there almost the entire population of Nagyvarad. The news of the finding of the shrine had aroused much interest. The superstitious were sure that the discovery of St. Ladislau's resting place meant nothing other than the good will of God toward Nagyvarad, and they wanted to be sure to see any miracles that were performed.

At the bottom of the old moat, soldiers were parading up and down on the thick, soft grass. Men of science were surveying the foundations which had been found under the fortress walls. We watched them for a while, and listened to Father as he explained everything to us, but soon I was no longer listening and was off again in my day dreams about flying. Here, where everyone was expecting a miracle, would be a splendid place to make the experiment.

On our return home I told Gergely to blow his horn at once, as a sign for a Club meeting. Soon the woodshed was overflowing with boys. When I announced my plan, they accepted it with enthusiasm. Then the question of a strong umbrella came up, and Lucas answered that he knew where we could get the largest and strongest umbrella in town— from Aunt Juli.

Aunt Juli was an apple woman who had her stand just behind our woodhouse. Like a monument, from morning until evening, she sat behind her little table on which were piled pyramids of apples. Never a smile crossed her serious face, as with one hand she held an apple up to the passerby and with the other she held high her dark blue umbrella. In winter time she had beneath the table a pot filled with coals, and she stopped from time to time to put on more coals, but in summer her only duty was to sell her apples and hold up the large umbrella—and keep one eye out for street boys. To her notion, boys were the worst creatures in the world. They were her principal customers, and she had ample opportunity to gather information regarding their habits.

Lucas's plan was simple. "We must surprise Aunt Juli," he said, "so that she will be obliged to let go of her umbrella for a moment. The next thing is for us to seize and hide it till we have made our experiment. After the parachute jump is over, we shall apologize to Aunt Juli and give back her umbrella."

It was not until late in the afternoon of the next day that we had a chance to approach Aunt Juli's stand unwatched. She had fallen asleep under the dazzling sun, but she still held tight to her umbrella. There she sat, with closed eyes. A peasant's ox-cart had been standing for a long time before her table. My brother Istvan crept close, a long cord dangling from his hand. He fastened one end to the ox-cart, the other end to the leg of Aunt Juli's table. Lucas was meanwhile lying on the roof of the woodhouse, just above Aunt Juli, waiting for the moment when she would release her hold on the umbrella. At last the owner of the ox-cart came out of a nearby grocery store, cracked his whip over his oxen, and shouted to them to move on. Aunt Juli woke to see her table, which had stood quietly before her for so many years, walk after the ox-cart. In that first moment, when her apples danced before her, she thought there was an earthquake, but when she saw the table move off as the wheels of the cart began to turn, she let out a yell like the roar of a female lion robbed of her cubs. Her eyes blazed with anger. In the next second she was rushing after her apples, and she had dropped her umbrella.

Like a well-trained actor, Lucas seized the umbrella and disappeared from the roof into the lot next door.

It was not until Aunt Juli had halted the peasant and his cart, recovered her table and dancing apples, and put them once more into their order of pyramid upon pyramid, that she remembered her umbrella. She stopped piling her apples, and stood meditating upon its disappearance. She looked up and down the street, to the right and to the left, but she could not find a clue. It could not have been stolen, since no one had been near her when she woke. And then the thought came to her of the miracle for which the whole city had been waiting since the discovery of the grave of St. Ladislau. Five minutes later everybody in Nagyvarad knew that Aunt Juli's umbrella had "vanished from sight while there were no people on the street"—a sign, certainly, of more miracles to come.

The next day was Sunday. Early in the afternoon I sent out two drummers and two trumpeters (the instruments had been borrowed from school for the summer vacation) to call an immediate gathering of the members of the Club. My brother Samuel had been sent to buy small, colored balloons which were intended not only to add color to my flight, but actually to help. It was our notion that we ought to attach the small balloons to the edge of the umbrella, in the event that it alone could not bring me down gracefully.

When we were ready to start, we sent the two trumpeters ahead with their high-voiced instruments, and after them came the drummers. Behind the musicians marched twelve boys in line, carrying twelve brightly-colored balloons. Behind them came Lucas, who bore on his shoulder Aunt Juli's umbrella, well wrapped. And on Lucas's heels I marched, the hero of the day, carrying in my pocket a big bunch of string. Now came the closed columns of the rest of our Club members and their small brothers.

We soon neared the place of the historical old fortress where, as it was a holiday, a tremendous crowd was gathered. The noise of our instruments and the shouts of our followers drew the attention of the people, and they crowded about to see what was happening. We had to push and shove to get to the place which I had chosen, but at last we stood on the margin of the deep trench where the old moat had been, and where now the soft green grass waved in the gentle west wind.

There we fastened to the edge of the opened umbrella the twelve colored balloons, which began a lively dance in the air. I did not wish to repeat the disaster that had occurred with my mother's umbrella, and that was why I had brought the pocket full of string. My idea was to fasten the tips of the ribs to the center stick and so keep the umbrella from turning right side out.

In such a crowd, however, it was impossible to work slowly and make sure that each cord was securely knotted; the boys were nervous, for they were being pushed and shoved, and they were afraid that they might go over into the trench. I was nervous too, as I jerked at the strings.

It was Lucas, who was more nervous than anyone, who was supposed to give me the final shove when the umbrella was ready. Before I had finished tying the strings, he thought I had given him the signal. By mere accident I looked up at him, and immediately he gave me a strong push. Over I went. I leapt clear of the embankment, holding desperately to the famous umbrella. Below me I saw the menacing depth. I had no time to prepare myself. Down I went, clinging like mad to the umbrella's handle, while the upper part with a great snap turned wrong side out. The only reason I was not injured seriously was because at the point where I landed the soldiers had been emptying garbage, and they had prepared a soft bed for me.

There I lay, too frightened and too dizzy even to look up. Some of the soldiers rushed to my aid, and when they helped me to my feet I found that my right ankle was in a bad way! They carried me to the army physician in the fortress, who bound up my ankle and gave me some distasteful though probably very sound advice on the avoidance of aeronautics.

Meanwhile the boys hung about the entrance of the fortress, wondering what had become of me but too frightened to inquire. Soon I appeared between two of the soldiers, who told the boys they would have to carry me home on their shoulders. They took turns. Lucas had the ruined umbrella under his arm. The musicians had no heart to attempt any more tunes.

As we straggled home by way of Inferno Street we must have been a pathetic sight after our brave outward march. And as we neared the corner nearest our house, we saw Aunt Juli, like an ancient fury, striding forward to meet us. She had heard of the reappearance of her precious lost umbrella. She tore the ruined treasure from Lucas's grasp, and began to divide among us the reward she thought we deserved. As fast as they could, the boys took to their heels, even the two who were at the moment carrying me, and I was left to face Aunt Juli's wrath alone.

It was Father, who had heard the noise and came running

out of the house, who saved me from Aunt Juli's vengeance. He promised her that he would see that we were all properly punished for our escapade, and that he would make full reparation for the umbrella, which promise somewhat soothed her so that she went back to her table and her apples, muttering curses upon the heads of all small boys.

MR. CHRISTMAS

Chapter Nine

AFTER THE shameful day of my flying experiment, we tried to be as good as it was possible for boys living by Inferno Street. I was condemned to be quiet through the long days because of my ankle, which proved to be badly sprained. The other boys could not stay beside me all the time, and so I spent many solitary hours in the woodhouse. My only amusement was to play the trumpet or to beat on the drum. This made life unbearable for Aunt Juli, who was seated only a foot away from the thin wall of our woodhouse. As the blasts of my trumpet arose, I could hear her shrill voice calling for the mercy of all the saints to stop my infernal racket. Her nerves, she declared, were wrecked entirely, and sometimes she threatened to see that the whole family was put out of the apartment immediately.

It was not long after my downfall with Aunt Juli's umbrella that a strange-looking man stopped at our house one afternoon. He said he wanted to speak to my father. Father was not at home, so I hobbled on my good foot into the kitchen and found Mother. Mother offered a seat to our visitor, who informed us that he was the landlord and that his name was Mr. Karacsony. The name translated into English would be Mr. Christmas.

Mr. Christmas was about seventy years old, six feet tall, and had a serious air and a long mustache. He was a veteran of the Solferino and the famous Königgrätz wars, where he served as sergeant of trumpeters in the Austrian army.

He told Mother immediately why he had come. He had had innumerable complaints about the behavior of the boys in our family, and he had been requested to force us out of our apartment. He said that the fact that Father, when he rented the rooms, misinformed him about the number in the family was sufficient reason to ask the court for an eviction.

My mother was not a good talker, and the landlord's accusation came so suddenly that she could find no excuses. As for me, when I realized that our guest brought no good news, I slipped out through the kitchen. To amuse myself, I took up our borrowed trumpet and tried, without much success, to play a famous soldiers' march which is used in every Hungarian regiment.

The false notes which I was drawing from the trumpet at last made Mr. Christmas so nervous that he said to my mother, "It's simply ear-splitting, the noise that boy makes."

Mother offered at once to silence me, but as she started to her feet, Mr. Christmas burst out in great indignation, "Don't stop him, Mrs. Finta. It isn't right to prevent boys from practicing on the trumpet. On the contrary, you must teach them to do it right." And striding to the door, he informed her that until my father's return home he would give me a lesson on the trumpet.

Mr. Christmas had long been a pensioned war veteran, and now lived the life of a lonely old bachelor. He had three small houses, and his only occupation was to collect the rents from his tenants. He had neither relatives nor friends, only an old dog. The moment I saw his tall heavy figure framed in the woodhouse doorway I thought to myself, "Now there will be a scolding!" But to my surprise, Mr. Christmas took my trumpet and began to show me how to hold the instrument correctly. His bent shoulders straightened, and he took the position of a soldier on parade. He drew a deep breath, and then began to play with great skill.

After Mr. Christmas had finished the march which I had struggled with so poorly, he handed the instrument to me and with the greatest of patience taught me how to stand, how to lift the trumpet, how to hold it, and how to blow if I wanted a clear, high tone. Between instructions he took the trumpet himself, and played many soldiers' marches.

My brothers heard the music and one by one drifted home

to stand silently in the door of the woodhouse listening to the landlord giving me my music lesson. The other boys of the neighborhood followed, and gathered in our yard.

When Mr. Christmas looked about at last, and saw the large number of boys inside and out, he asked whether summer school was just out.

"No," I said, "these are my brothers, here, and the rest are our friends."

"If that is true," said Mr. Christmas, "then your father is the biggest liar in the world. When he rented this house, he told me he had one adopted child, an orphan boy."

"That's so, Mr. Christmas," I replied. "We have an orphan boy, and also two girls and seven boys, and we have fifty-two members in our Club."

His eyes opened in amazement, and after a little consideration, he said more to himself than to me, "So many boys and nobody to teach them discipline. Line up!" commanded Mr. Christmas, and when the boys had obeyed this sudden command, he ordered me to blow the soldiers' march that he had just been teaching me.

While I played he arranged the boys in columns, showing them how to stand straight, and how to keep in step. The air was filled with his orders, sharply given, a pleasanter sound in the ears of the passersby than the usual noise that rose in our yard.

That evening when my father arrived home he stopped in his tracks, astounded by the spectacle which greeted him. A tall, white-haired man, carrying his walking stick like a sword, was standing in the middle of the court giving commands, and we boys were marching around the yard in orderly lines.

When Mr. Christmas saw Father he stopped the drill, dismissed each column one after another, but ordered every boy to report the next afternoon. Father, Mr. Christmas, and we six boys went into the house. Mother had set the table for dinner, and she invited Mr. Christmas to be our guest.

He was tired from the drill, and hungry. And he said he had some more things to tell us concerning the art of trumpeting, so he accepted Mother's invitation and stayed. As soon as dinner was over, Father, who was always forthright in such things, asked Mr. Christmas why he had come to visit us.

At Father's question, Mr. Christmas moved uneasily upon his chair. When she saw him hesitate, Mother helped him out, explaining in her gentle way that Mr. Christmas had been asked to evict us because we had such a large family. Before she could finish, our landlord broke in with, "I think those differences can be straightened out with a little good will," and immediately began to talk of something else.

Mr. Christmas lived in one of his houses on the other side of the Koros River. He had always hated the walk to the house where we were living because of the long zigzag way along Inferno Street, but after that day when he had come with the intention of putting us out, he visited us frequently. At last he moved into an apartment in the house where we lived and settled there permanently with his old dog, Csimbok. When those who had asked him to evict us would question his change of heart, his answer would be abrupt: "Somebody must teach those boys discipline!"

We boys were delighted and immediately elected him Commander-in-Chief and life member of our Club. From that day on the old veteran had no leisure time. Besides teaching us to play the trumpet, and to drill, he had daily to act as the arbiter of our quarrels, for to us he had become the judge of the court of last appeal, and we took his judgment as absolute and perfect in all things.

THE FUNERAL SINGERS

Chapter Ten

WE HAD GOOD singing voices, my brothers and I, and often we were called by a funeral director, Mr. Weislovits, to a cemetery in the neighborhood of our street to sing at funerals. This created a certain respect for us, but what seemed bigger in our eyes, it was also profitable. We were earning money during summer vacation.

Some people make a living by exploiting physical strength or superior mentality; Mr. Weislovits's talent was different. He could yield genuine tears at a moment's notice. He would stand at the door of his funeral establishment, watching for someone to pass by dressed in mourning garb. At once his voice would change from its natural tone and he would greet

them with tears, and it would have taken an attentive observer
to notice that his feeling was interest in his business, not sympathy for his neighbor. His greeting almost invariably began
in the same way:

"He died? . . . oh, he was a good man, an excellent father.
He merits a nice funeral, a first class one."

If he had made a mistake and the customer had to correct
him with, "Oh, Mr. Weislovits, the one who died wasn't a
he but a she," this never bothered him. He went on at once,
"Oh, oh! She really was a good mother, and she merits a nice
funeral, a very nice one!" At this point he would pull out his
large handkerchief and try to stop the tears which were flow-
ing down his cheeks, but he was never able to check them
until he had reached an agreement with the mourner.

So his enterprise went on with success. He grew rich, and
when the city council auctioned off an old theater building in
our end of the town, Mr. Weislovits bought it at a bargain
and moved his business into it. At first the whole town
laughed at him, but their ridicule only served to advertise his
business, which daily grew bigger and more elaborate.

At the funeral hall, what had once been the theater gallery
was filled with caskets in the latest styles. But Mr. Weislovits
was too old and too busy to climb up to the gallery every day
to dust his large stock of caskets, so he engaged me and my
brothers, who had served him so often as funeral singers, to
go up there and do the cleaning.

At first we felt queer walking about among so many new
coffins, and we talked to each other in whispers. Later on,
however, we grew so used to it that we actually came to like
our job, especially since Mr. Weislovits was very generous in

the matter of tips, which he called "zulaug." School had begun again, but every day after classes were over, we stopped
by the old theater to clean the funeral parlor and do anything
else the old gentleman wanted.

One day, when Mr. Weislovits was interviewing some visitors who had just lost a rich relative, we saw that he was weeping without much result. The visitors could have afforded a
first class funeral, but they were stingy and resisted all Mr.
Weislovits's suggestions. We felt that we ought to assist our
employer, so all at once we joined in with Mr. Weislovits's
sobs. This surprised the visitors so that they asked, "Why do
you cry?"

I replied for the four of us, "We cannot bear to see Mr.
Weislovits shedding so many tears and getting no business
in return."

For a moment Mr. Weislovits stopped crying, and as he
turned on us we saw his eyes flash like a tiger's, though he ad-
dressed his guests in the sweetest voice imaginable. "You see,
even these innocent boys are deeply touched by the sorrowful event."

After the customers had gone, however, he turned on us in
a rage, and would have discharged us on the spot, if we had not
promised never again to loiter around when a customer
arrived.

After that, we knew when a customer was coming by the
energetic motions of Mr. Weislovits in our direction, which
meant, "Get out and stay out!" If we did not disappear at
once, then we received no zulaug for that day.

One afternoon, as it was getting late, my brother Istvan
and I were in the gallery dusting when we saw Mr. Weis-

lovits and several peasant customers almost upon us. We had no choice but to hide, and the only place we could see at the moment was one of the large wooden caskets. We just had time to crawl inside when we heard them stop beside the coffin.

"Isn't this a beautiful piece of funeral furniture?" spoke Mr. Weislovits in his sad business tones. "Really, he was good hearted, and deserves just such a fine coffin as this. Oh, how he would rest in it!"

At that moment someone called from below that Mr. Weislovits was wanted urgently, and he had to leave his customers alone. The peasants tried by lifting the coffins to find the one most solidly built. Naturally the one we were in was the heaviest. When Mr. Weislovits returned they had agreed among themselves that they would take the coffin in which we were hidden! "And we shall take it with us now," they told him.

"I will fasten it for you," he said, "and you can carry it to your wagon." Whereupon with a jerk he snapped down four strong locks and we were prisoners. We lay quietly inside, hoping for some miraculous salvation once we were outside the funeral hall. The coffin was large enough for two slender boys, but we were almost suffocated. Luckily it was really not very well made, and some of the wood had warped. At several places the joining had wide spaces through which a little air came in, and we could see some light; but though we put our eyes to the slits again and again we could see nothing outside.

At first we did not consider our plight very serious or dangerous, and we could not resist chuckling over the shrewdness of the peasants who thought they had bought the best coffin because it was the heaviest.

As they placed it on the wagon they spoke of getting home to the funeral feast. Even today, it is the custom in Hungary to hold a rich feast whenever some adult member of the family dies. This custom goes back to the time when the Hungarians were a nomadic people wandering out of Asia. Then, after a death, all relatives and friends of the deceased, and often even those who were his enemies in this life would gather at the feast, and it often happened that these gatherings became so expensive that they absorbed all the inheritance.

Istvan and I could not expect to be welcome guests at this particular funeral feast, and we discussed in whispers how we should escape the moment the coffin was opened. For until it was unloaded from the cart and the locks unfastened, there was nothing we could do.

In the coffin were placed some long sheets of paper, to protect the inner surface. We agreed that upon the lifting of the lid, we would each cover ourselves with one of these sheets, and drawing it about us like the hood of a ghost, make a dive through the crowd and so escape, as swiftly as possible.

Our uneasiness grew as time passed and we still rumbled on. We kept asking each other, "How does a ghost really behave? Can we do it?" If we could not frighten the peasants, would they let us go in peace anyway?

At length we heard the barking of many dogs who seemed to be circling the cart in welcome. This was a new danger. The one hope we had was that the peasants would open the coffin the moment they reached their journey's end, but now, hearing those dogs, we thought perhaps we were safer inside.

We knew by the dimness of the light through the slit that the sun was gone, and it was growing dark; we would not get home by nightfall now. We did not care about that. All we wanted was to be left safe within the coffin until those terrible dogs had gone to sleep or had wandered off at some distance.

We knew now where we were, for we had heard one of the peasants name the village. It was Szaldobagy, on the outskirts of Nagyvarad, and we knew too, that John Kovats, the stingiest bachelor in that small place, was laid out in state, waiting for his coffin. Part of the story we read in the paper later on; Kovats had no family or close relatives, but lived alone with his chickens and his geese and other fancy poultry which were his pride and only pleasure. The day before he had been found by his neighbors lying on his kitchen doorstep.

Hearing the news, the mayor of the little village ordered the distant relatives, who had none too much sympathy for the stingy old man, to decide at once about his funeral, and sent some of them to town to buy the coffin, while the others prepared for the ceremony. While the two peasants had been in Nagyvarad, all the neighbors and relatives, and even those who had barely spoken to Kovats in his life, had gathered at the house for the traditional funeral feast.

It was the chickens, doubtless, that most regretted Kovats's departure, for they became the victims for the celebration of the sad event. Mercilessly one after another was slaughtered as more and more guests arrived, and the chimney smoked as it never had done in all Kovats's lifetime, and as few chimneys in the neighborhood ever smoked, for all the inhabitants of Szaldobagy were poor and lived modestly.

Kovats, too, had wine in his cellar. Not much, to be sure, but what he had was old and of the best quality, and while the women cooked the feast, the men found amusement in tasting the various kinds and comparing their flavors. From then on, their voices grew louder, as they told and retold the life story of Kovats, which after all was not so different from the life of anyone in that village.

When the men who had returned with the coffin reached the place, the air was already rich with the pleasant odor of roasting chicken. The cart had barely stopped within the yard when they chased off the dogs and without unfastening the coffin locks hurried in to share in the fine dinner.

First the feast comes, then the mourning. This is the way it goes in Hungary, and the people like it so. We lay for a long time in our hiding place, but soon the dogs came back to sniff at the box, barking and leaping upon it, and we trembled. They only left us when someone called them to get the scraps in the kitchen. When we were sure we were once more alone in the dark, I took it upon myself to reassure Istvan. After all I was the older.

"Don't worry," I said. "We will escape those dogs."

"I hope so," was the whispered reply.

Nothing lasts forever in this world, not even a good dinner. But it must have been midnight when we heard heavy steps approaching; we had been almost asleep from weariness and suffocation, but now I roused my brother, and in a low voice told him to take hold of one of the paper sheets and be ready to run the instant the coffin lid was lifted.

We felt the coffin lifted and carried, and then it was set upon a floor. Through the widest slit I thought I could see the wooden horses, upon which the coffin was to stand, being prepared in the kitchen. The peasant's house generally consists of two rooms separated by a third, the kitchen. The larger room is what is known as the "clean" room, and is used only when there are visitors, or upon special occasions. The other is the bedroom, or "back" room, and living and cooking and eating and work are all done in the kitchen.

When the large gathering had finished their dinner, the smell of which made our mouths water, they cleared a space of tables and pots and dishes, and set up the stand for the coffin, so that all the feasters might look their last upon Kovats. They made a stand of two heavy wooden horses, covered with a wide black cloth that reached to the ground. They lighted two long wax candles and stood them at the end of the bier. All this they made ready with great solemnity.

One of the two peasants who had brought the coffin stepped forward and announced, "It is I who shall be funeral master."

The crowd, which until now had been a noisy one, stopped talking, and even their pipes left their mouths for a short interval. They pushed into the kitchen, pressing themselves against the wall to leave room in the middle for the funeral master and his helpers.

When the two strongest, at the request of the master, lifted the coffin from the ground, our hearts leapt into our throats. The moment had come. The coffin settled into place upon the black-covered horses, the locks were snapped up, the lid was lifted. . . .

I had seized one of the paper sheets upon which we had been lying; Istvan had seized the other. The next moment Istvan made a leap for the left side of the box, and I made a

leap in the other direction, but something jerked us back into the box. For a moment we were both paralyzed by this unexpected frustration of our plans, then we tried once more, and the sheet of paper, which we had thought to be in two pieces, gave a loud tearing sound, and parted down the middle where it had been folded and fitted into the coffin.

At our first struggles with the snow-white sheet, the visitors, who had drunk long and deeply, stood as if stupefied. As we rose, still dragging at the paper which waved above our heads, their eyes grew so large that their broad peasant faces almost disappeared. Then, as the sheet tore apart with a loud ripping noise, we almost fell from the coffin and into the midst of that stricken crowd.

The sheets floated stiffly in the air above us like two out-stretched wings, and rustled as we dodged about, trying to find a way to leave. My first move had been toward the small back room, but that way was blocked by two pall bearers carrying Kovats, who, appalled by the apparition of two flapping pairs of wings, dropped their burden upon the ground.

Istvan by this time was headed for the kitchen door, and I turned about and ran after him. We fled flapping and rustling into the night, and not one of the awe-stricken peasants dared to follow.

It was almost dawn when, dog-tired from our adventure, we tiptoed into our house, and slipped into bed. Next day in answer to Mother's questions we said that we had been invited to assist at the opening of the new theater, which kept us very late. She was proud of her boys, and thought this was none too remarkable, that they should be asked to be present at an important event.

What was our amazement, however, on our way to school, to find that every newspaper in town was full of last night's adventure. We read eagerly. "TWO WHITE-WINGED ANGELS WORK MIRACLE" ran the headlines. What could it mean? Kovats, the papers said, was alive. We looked at each other and read on.

The two pall bearers admitted that they had let him fall to the ground, but that was part of the miracle. Kovats then told his part of the story. The night of his "death" he had been sitting on the back steps eating his supper. Some yolk of a hard-boiled egg had lodged in his throat and choked him, and he had gone into a faint which his neighbors had mistaken for death. For two days he had remained unconscious. The jolt when the two bearers dropped him must have dislodged the piece of food, said Kovats, and the breath had rushed back into his lungs.

Now the other guests gave their share of the details. While they were still thunder-struck by the apparition of two angels leaping from the coffin, they heard the voice of the dead man. Trembling, they turned in his direction. He was sitting upright, holding his aching throat and asking in a husky voice, "What's this? What's going on here?"

He rose from the ground, and walked about his own bier, putting out his hands to touch everything, to see if it was real. His slow walk, his silent curiosity, paralyzed the funeral guests.

Then he smelled the rich odor of cooked chicken, and he knew he had really come back to this life. He was hungry! And he had fasted for two days.

He turned to the master of ceremonies, who stood like a stone carving, immobile from dread. Kovats's tone was one of eager curiosity. "Did you have a chicken dinner?"

"Yes," breathed the master of ceremonies.

"May I have a bite of the chicken paprika?" asked the revived in an anguish of eagerness.

"No, we didn't leave a bite."

"Have you killed all my rare poultry?"

"Not one is left," came the frightened answer.

"And have you finished all my fine wine, too?"

"Nearly, yes."

And then, according to the newspaper, Mr. Kovats, the stingiest bachelor in Hungary, leaned upon his coffin and burst into bitter tears.

Istvan and I never knew whether Mr. Weislovits connected us with the strange happenings at Kovats's, or with the subsequent returning of the wooden coffin, for we never returned to the funeral parlor. The zulaug, we decided, was not worth the risk one ran in such a business!

BIG GAME HUNTERS GO INTO TRAINING

Chapter Eleven

I WAS NOW registered in the real Gymnasium, where I elected mechanics as my special study. In my mechanics class I became acquainted with a bright fellow named Ludwig Nagy, whose father was an inspector on the estate of Count Richard Redey, an Hungarian aristocrat. Ludwig and I became very close friends. He sat beside me in class, and we shared fortunes and misfortunes.

I spent the Christmas vacation on the large farm where his father was overseer, and we had a fine holiday, most of the time riding on horseback through the thick woods that covered the hillsides. It was then that we planned to hold a big hunting party at the end of the school year.

The forest which surrounded the Redey estate was called Vercsorog, which means in English "Bloodpour" because it

was here that the Magyars in conquering Hungary cut into
the retreating army of Men-Maroth. This forest was still
mostly in its natural state, and was full of bears, wolves, foxes,
and other big-game animals. This plan occupied our imaginations for the rest of the school year.

It was our ambition to shoot a huge wild boar—as big as we
could find—and to make from his tusks decorated charms for

our watch chains. We meant to carve on the tusks the date when the dangerous boar had fallen under our blows.

We saved every cent we could collect during the second semester and willingly accepted any and all jobs, no matter how dirty, to earn a little money to invest in hunters' knives, and any other equipment which we thought might be useful.

We calculated the chances of meeting a bear, and we planned daily exercises to strengthen our muscles against the time when we might be attacked by one at the same moment when we were overcoming a boar. Every afternoon we met upon the banks of the Koros River and invented a game in which different boys represented bears, boars, and wolves. With the eager help of Csimbok, Mr. Christmas's dog, we strove to perfect our skill in the art of big-game hunting.

We seriously discussed every possibility, and in the last week before our summer vacation we decided that, to defend ourselves in any kind of attack from a bear, we should become skilled ax throwers. We immediately bought five middle-sized hatchets, and every day we went to the near-by woods where we had set up a bear's silhouette cut from cardboard, and there we practiced "hitting the bear" for hours at a time. Even after considerable effort, we found it was not so easy to hit him in a vulnerable spot every time. This was a bit disappointing, but we did not let it interfere with our larger plans, for we were quite nonchalant about our skill.

Under pretext that we must study for the week of examinations that was upon us, we persuaded Mother to help us get away from our small brothers, who otherwise followed our every step. And so we had a whole week of daily practice in the dangerous art of throwing the knife and ax. When

the school year was really done, we felt ourselves well prepared for the long dreamed-of hunt.

Our big secret aroused eager interest in the suspicious minds
of our little brothers who had not been allowed to play with
us. Toward the end of our preparations, they tried harder
and harder to follow us and learn what we were doing.

The second week after examinations were over, I begged
Father to allow us to go for a week's vacation to our Uncle
Moses, who had a small farm in a village not far from Nagyvarad. And after much urging, he consented. It was my secret
plan that first we should go to Vercsorog for the long-planned
hunt, and from there we would go to Uncle Moses' farm
where we would stay for a day or two.

The day before our departure, we were so nervous that we
almost lost our senses. I had the greatest difficulty in keeping
Lucas out of the house that day, for I knew that he would
never be able to keep our secret from Mother and the small
boys. Mother did not approve of our father's decision to let
us go on the vacation without the younger ones.

By suppertime we brothers were so nervous we could not
touch a bite of food; Lucas, however, was quite cheerful and
unconcerned. But what surprised me was that our little brothers
asked us no questions about our plans for the trip to the farm.
They ate their suppers with their usual good appetites, and
as soon as possible went off to bed and to sleep. We older
boys sat up for a long time, listening to Father's careful instructions about the road to Ujlak where Uncle Moses lived.
He also cautioned us to be on our guard against wayside dogs.
We exchanged amused glances when Father recommended
that we each carry a walking stick for our self defense.

I felt that the responsibility for the success of our adventure lay on my shoulders. Sleep came to me only fitfully, and I was awake long before sunrise. Cautiously, I woke my three brothers and Lucas. In the dark we took up our clothes, which Mother had mended and laid out for us, and bundling them under our arms, tiptoed down the stairs and out through the courtyard. We were afraid to dress in our room for fear of waking our younger brothers.

What was our astonishment after all our careful plans, to find our little brothers sitting on top of the wood pile under which we had hidden our provisions for the trip. There they were, all dressed, and with the sweetest of smiles wreathing their rosy cheeks. They immediately assured me that they would be my best helpers in the big game hunt in the big forest. Turning on Lucas I accused him of treachery.

He admitted it cheerfully. "I did tell the little rascals a few things," he said, "but not everything."

I thought for a moment and decided that an immediate refusal would only bring howls, and perhaps Father or Mother would come down to find out what was the matter, and so the whole secret would be out and that would mean more disappointment for us. I knew that by the time I was dressed I would have thought up some way to escape from this predicament. "You can go," I said, "if you are willing to carry the supplies for our camp." They agreed willingly.

We took from the hiding place all our supplies, and I conceived an idea for losing the youngsters then and there. As soon as we older boys were dressed, we bound to our own shoulders the hatchets, the lassos, and all the equipment without which we knew we could never bring down any big game. As I was busy with the cords, I whispered my plan into their ears, except for Lucas, who would have given me away by demanding that I "speak louder." When we were all ready, I cut two long pieces of cord and tied bundles of shovels, axes, brooms, and two stout logs upon the backs of the two small boys. As soon as their heavy bundles were in place, at my signal, we laid both Arpad and Mateh upon the floor, pulled off their shoes, and ran out of the door as fast as we could go, leaving them to their fate. We tossed the shoes upon the woodhouse roof as we left, and soon we had put them a long way behind us.

We had decided earlier to avoid Inferno Street and to take the longer way to the Koros River Bridge. With long strides and gay talk we neared the bridge, all of us feeling satisfied with our trick and glad that in this big adventure the small boys would be safe at home in the care of Mother. But when we neared the narrow planking of the bridge, there stood Arpad, my eight-year-old brother. Mother had heard their shouts, and had released Arpad, who was the most determined to go along with us.

Arpad knew through Lucas that we had no intention of going to Ujlak, and that we were taking the longest route out of the city, so he raced along Inferno Street, which was almost empty of people so early in the morning. And as he had hoped, he reached the bridge ahead of us and waited our arrival.

For a moment we were speechless when we recognized our barefooted Arpad, standing like a statue on the end of the bridge. His face was proud and smiling as the full moon when he caught sight of us. We stopped and put down our burdens, and I tried to persuade him to go home, but without success.

I even offered him my brand-new hunting knife, and I promised that when we came back I would teach him to throw it, and to throw a hatchet, but all to no avail. At last I ordered Lucas, who was the sinner who had created this whole state of affairs, to take all the responsibility for Arpad throughout the journey. Then we took up our bundles to start on again, only to discover that Arpad, in his race down Inferno Street, had stubbed his big toe and hurt it badly. His foot was covered with blood, and after examining the toe I found that he had lost his toenail. Istvan, who had had first aid training at school, took him down to the river bed and there washed and bandaged the wound.

Lucas remarked as we started on, "Well, we've caught a lame duck already. We're pretty good hunters." But the rest of us didn't think that so very funny.

The first hours of our march took us far along the way. Arpad even with his sore toe walked bravely forward until the sun had climbed to the top of the sky. Then the hot road began to burn the bottoms of his bare feet, and he complained of the pain. We stopped and fashioned some sandals for him from a piece of cloth, and for a while again he bore up well. We had to keep moving right ahead, for it was sixteen miles to the farm where my friend Ludwig and his parents lived. The last quarter of our journey was through the deep forest where we had ridden and made our plans at Christmas time.

Our difficulties increased with the passing hours. Little Arpad with his sore toe could hardly keep up with our pace. The sun grew more and more dazzling; and in the middle of July the open road exposed us to a heat quite different from anything we had ever experienced. From time to time we were forced to stop. We tried helping Arpad to walk, one on each side, but with little success. Early in the afternoon we faced the shame and disappointment of having to return home, for Arpad all at once refused to go another step.

A Rumanian peasant driving a small wagon pulled up at the side of the road where we were all gathered about Arpad. I told him that our brother had had an accident, and could go no further. He kindly gave us a lift, and on we went in the rumbling peasant cart. Traveling six miles at such a pace was agony for me, worse than going on foot, but for Arpad and his sore toe it was the only solution.

It was not long before we saw ahead of us the forest, and the fork in the road where our cart and the friendly peasant would leave us. We must make the rest of the journey on foot.

THE BIG GAME HUNT

Chapter Twelve

WHEN THE Rumanian peasant left us, we were still a fair distance from Ludwig Nagy's home. It was growing late, and the man advised us to make haste, lest we be overtaken by the storm which was threatening, and be forced to spend the night in the woods.

We did our best, thinking when once we had entered the forest to find it cool under the protection of the big trees, and not so wearisome as the long hot road. But that day it was our misfortune to find no air whatever in the narrow road through the woods. It was damp and hot, so that we felt a struggle for breath, and our energies were soon sapped. We had penetrated into the woods about three miles when we realized that our strength was almost exhausted, and knew we should not be able to get through before sunset.

Istvan and I began to worry, for we knew night dropped suddenly in such dense woods beyond the mountains. Then Arpad commenced to cry and declared again that he could go no farther, so I commanded that we stop for a long rest.

We had scarcely laid aside our heavy packs when a wind began to shake the leaves, the sunlight faded, and sudden darkness fell under the trees. I jumped to my feet and ordered the boys into action, for I knew danger lurked in a thunderstorm which covered the sun so rapidly and set the forest to creaking and groaning in a moment. My own fatigue vanished with the realization of our peril. I ordered the boys to shoulder their packs at once, and, leaving the forest road, we descended into a deep valley where we found a small brook. I decided that this was the place to spend the night.

We took a long, cool drink, and I divided our small supply of food, giving larger portions to the two younger boys, Arpad and Lucas. After this sketchy meal, I began to look about for quarters that would protect us from the oncoming night and storm, and chose at last a big oak tree with many strong branches. We took our hatchets, and climbing into the branches of the tree, we made a large nest about the trunk,

weaving in and out the smaller branches which we had cut off. It made an excellent flooring for our airy place.

We were on the ground collecting our packs when such a gust of wind bowed the crests of the trees that we were almost unable to climb up into our oak. The rest of us could have made it if it had not been for Arpad, who was worn out from his day-long trot to keep up with our strides, and from the heat and excitement.

We finally agreed on a plan; three of the boys were to climb into the nest around the trunk, and by the aid of the lassos, which we fixed under Arpad's arm, they were to pull him up, while Lucas and I stayed on the ground to steady their human freight until it was in the tree. But when we attempted it, we were all too weak and tired. At last I had to climb up into the tree and help pull, and it was only with the greatest difficulty that the four of us succeeded in pulling him into the nest. We bound him as securely as we could to the trunk, and he soon fell asleep.

Struggling against the onslaughts of the wind, we descended once more—it was a good twenty feet from our nest to the ground—and cut larger branches which we pulled up and set about our platform, making it more secure.

A flash of lightning was followed by a thunder-clap which shook the thick air, and was followed in turn by a tremendous wind plowing through the dense thicket, which gave rise to so many groans and cries in the forest that we clambered up into the tree as fast as we could go.

Another flash illuminated the forest, and for a moment blinded us. I counted ten between the flash and the thunder, and so I knew that the storm was still a long way off, but I feared it was traveling directly toward us and would last a long time.

We kept busy making every preparation for security and shelter. There was a tent in our baggage, and with the ropes we had intended for lassos, we fastened the tent to the branches above us, which bent and groaned under the constant pressure of the violent wind. We covered Arpad with blankets to protect him from rain; lying in a huddle, he slept the sleep of utter exhaustion. And now the rain poured down.

We older boys tried to settle ourselves to sleep also, but the moment we grew drowsy a thunderbolt would jolt us awake. I felt responsible for everything that had happened, and tried to encourage the others by telling them how much more violent the storms were on the plains, in those years when I had been a herdboy with my Uncle Miklos. I told them that anyone who rode through such a storm on the back of a frightened horse was in much more danger than we, in our well-built nest.

My talk was cut short in that very second by a bolt of lightning which struck a tree only a short distance from ours. The boys almost leapt from the nest in terror. Luckily the cords with which we had tied ourselves to the branches had gradually tightened as they grew wetter, and held us fast. The air smelled of sulphur from the bolt, and the storm raged on all about us.

The rumbling of thunder and the crash of falling trees drove the wild animals of the forest from their hiding places and they rushed from one shelter to another. In their panic they were blindly staggering against rock and bush and tree in their search for protection. Our valley was only one of many filled with rushing water, cutting animals off their regular trails.

Our innocent little brook raged now, and in the flashes we saw it tumbling rocks down its streambed as though they had been pebbles, and still the waters rose.

We clung together, and for a while thought we were lost in the furious tumult, for in that roar every other sound was drowned out. In the midst of chaos, we felt something fall heavily into our oak and stop among the branches a little way over our heads.

Then, in a last wild whirlwind, the storm blew itself out. The flashes came only at intervals, the thunder-claps long after. The storm had moved on. As the forest grew less tumultuous, we heard a painful voice crying overhead. It was a strange voice, puzzling to us all, for we could not tell whether it was human or animal, and it seemed to share a bit of both qualities.

The quieter the forest grew, the clearer we heard that strange cry from above, and still we could not decide what it could be. We tried to sleep, soaked to the skin though we were, but every time we snatched a bit of a nap, that desperate cry of the creature above would rouse us.

By daybreak our necks were stiff from bending back as we tried to peer into the branches overhead, and to make some shape of the thing that cried there in the tree. A thick mist had settled after the storm had passed, but when the sun broke through and we knew it was getting light, I decided to make my way into the treetop and find out what it was that made such agonized cries.

Sticking my hatchet into my belt, I slowly began to climb up and up the wet trunk of the tree. At last I could see what it was that had kept us awake until dawn; an eagle, imprisoned

in the thick branches. The terrible storm had blown it into a crotch of the tree, and held it there so that it could not use its wings. It was a prisoner indeed.

I saw that it was a king eagle, one of the largest birds in Hungary, which makes its nest among the rocks of the mountains and is famous for its size, its strength, and its boldness. Reports come occasionally that this eagle kidnaps children at play about their cottages and carries them off to its nest in the high pinnacles of the hills.

When I recognized that our ancient oak had captured such a prize for us, I almost lost my balance and tumbled to the ground. I had sense enough left, however, to climb back to our platform and get a rope. My brothers watched me eagerly, but I told them nothing, and clambered up again. With the greatest care I put a loop about the bird's legs just above those mighty talons. It moved, trying to strike at me, and I was fearful of being clawed or bitten, but the crotch of the tree held it too cramped for that. Once the legs were bound I tied the wings securely with my handkerchief. When I was certain that the king eagle was in my power, I cut off the limb which held the bird prisoner.

The eagle had fallen with its wings stretched upward, so it took me some little time to chop away the encircling branches. The head turned, as the thicket lessened, and the beak missed my fingers only by inches. So I pulled off one of my socks and drew it over the bird's head to blind it.

At last I had it in my arms, strong, struggling, eager to be free. I managed to drop myself limb by limb into the reach of the eager boys below. They showered me with questions I had no breath to answer.

"Be careful," I said, lowering the precious burden into their outstretched arms. "It is a king eagle, a living king eagle."

They were too thunderstruck to reply. We lowered it to the ground finally and examined it. The wings must have had a spread of ten feet and more across. It was a splendid specimen, healthy, and as hungry as we were.

I set two of the boys to guard the great bird of prey and the rest of us moved our possessions down from our aerial castle. They were in an ecstasy over the turn fortune had taken, and scrambled gaily up and down, chattering all the while.

The woods around Vercsorog were the home of the strawberry, and we found berries in abundance, but so battered by the storm that hardly one was fit to eat. We mostly searched for blackberries, for they are a hardier fruit and will stand more buffeting.

When the edge was taken from our hunger we set out to find some food for our eagle. Lucas and Arpad agreed to guard the bird, and we three older boys put our belts about our waists, stuck our knives and hatchets into them, and set out to hunt in earnest.

The small brook near our tree, which in the early morning had been overflowing its banks, gradually receded to its regular bed, but the soil under the tree was still wet, and we were able to advance only by taking long leaps from stone to stone, or from hillock to hillock. We held our hands on our hatchets, and watched in every direction, so as not to be taken by surprise. Istvan felt courageous, and going ahead of us, he penetrated the first screen of thick bushes. Soon we heard a cry of surprise in his direction, and we followed where he had gone. He turned a white face to us and his voice trembled as he told us he had seen a huge animal—an elephant, or something like it.

We went into a long conference, during which time any sort of animal, even a tortoise, could have escaped. Then we decided to go forward in a line, slowly, and attack the animal from all sides at once.

Slowly, very slowly, we drew our line forward, step by step. At last Istvan cried loudly, "There it is, there it is!"

The monster which faced us, his mouth open, his great tusks pointed in our direction, was a boar, the biggest boar, I am certain, in all the neighborhood of Vercsorog. We did not move, however, and still keeping at a safe distance, we marched around the beast inspecting him with wonder.

We realized at last that he was dead, and then we all had some explanation to offer as to how the accident had happened. Probably the right one was that in the terrible storm he had been caught in a landslide and thrown down the steep hillside, and had broken his neck. He had landed upright in such a lifelike pose in the middle of the briars that even a trained hunter might have been wary of approaching.

The suggestions about what to do with him now that we had found him were as numerous as the speculations as to what had happened to him. At last we decided to cut off the big tusks first as an everlasting proof of our bravery, and leave the decision of what to do with the body to the family of Ludwig Nagy.

I examined the jaws and decided I could chop out the tusks. My sharp little hatchet glittered in the sunshine, and each stroke echoed through the silence of the forest. Scarcely had we lifted the two heavy tusks to our shoulders when we heard the distress call on our trumpet. Lucas had blown it badly, but it told us that something had happened around our camp.

Our minds flew to our precious prisoner, the king eagle. We ran toward camp, spattering through the mud which almost tore our shoes from our feet.

THE BIRD COLLECTION
OF VERCSOROG

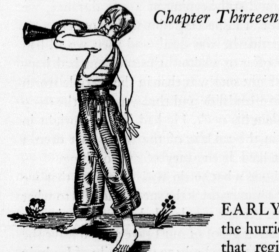

Chapter Thirteen

EARLY ON the day after the hurricane had swept over that region, Count Richard Redey, the owner of the estate about Vercsorog, drove through the woods in his light chaise, to see what damage the terrible storm had done. His inspection tour was halted by a tree which had fallen near our camp and blocked the narrow road through the woods. He tied up his horse, and started to inspect that part of the woods, fearing that more of his century-old trees had been torn up.

When he reached the narrow valley and the brook near our oak tree camp, he was astonished to see some of our clothing, which had been spread to dry, waving like small flags on the bushes. Camps were so rare in that remote spot that he began at once to search about and soon came upon little Arpad and Lucas, searching for berries.

He asked them what their business was in his wood.

Lucas replied promptly, "We are in search of big game."

"What did you say?" demanded the Count in amusement. "In search of big game? In these woods?"

"Yes," replied Lucas with his usual nonchalance. "We came just for that reason, and we have had some success already."

He took Count Redey to where the eagle sat hunched and silent, and pulled off my sock which had blinded it. But the very second the blindfold was removed, the eagle began to shriek with all its strength.

The Count had never been more amazed in all his life. He started back, and looked at the big bird as if he could not believe his eyes. He was a bachelor, and had spent his life in solitude here on his estate in the lonely woods and mountains of Hungary, and his great hobby and amusement had been the collecting of birds that lived on his lands. He had already a great number of interesting specimens in his castle, some caged, and some at large in the courtyard. He had never, however, been able to capture a king eagle, one of the rarest birds in the country. And here was a little boy casually introducing him to one.

When Lucas had put the blindfold back upon the eagle—and with great care because of that terrible beak—Count Redey inquired again what he and Arpad were doing there.

Lucas was glad to make conversation, and told him that he had come with his brothers, who were now out in the woods hunting for boars and bears and wolves. "They took their hatchets with them," he said, "and their gun." He didn't mention that the gun was only a toy. "And I think they had their hunters' knives and lassos, didn't they, Arpad?"

"Of course," agreed Arpad eagerly. "And they left us to guard the king eagle."

The Count wondered whether he had met with the dwarfs which the peasants believed in and talked about endlessly, or whether he was merely dreaming a fantastic fairy tale. "Where are your brothers?" he asked.

"I can call them," Lucas offered, and he took up the trumpet and blew the signal for us to come.

We appeared at last, and fearful that something had attacked Lucas and Arpad, we came each with his hatchet in his hand, and Istvan and I brandishing knives, with the boar tusks between us.

On beholding this second miracle, the Count could not speak.

Lucas was equal to any occasion. "Did I not tell you? Here are the boar's tusks. Next will come the bear's claws. Now will you believe your eyes?"

The Count looked at us with wonder in his face; six children armed with sharp hatchets, in an abandoned part of the wild forest, being the possessors of two such champion trophies, was almost unbelievable. And then he began to laugh.

He sat down on the ground and held his sides. At first we were insulted that he should take our adventure so lightly, but after a few moments his laugh sounded so hearty and so full of good fellowship that we joined in.

"Sit here beside me," he said when he could speak, "and tell me all about it."

The six of us formed a circle about him, and with some help from the others, I told the story, beginning with our plan to visit Ludwig Nagy, the son of Count Redey's inspector.

"Yes," nodded the Count. "I know him. I am the Count, you know, and all these forests are mine."

We burst into laughter at that. "You, a count? A Hungarian count? No sir, you can't fool us. We know what a count looks like, for we have seen pictures of them in our books at school. You might be his valet, but Count Redey certainly looks very different."

"Well, well, it doesn't matter. Go on with your story."

I told him then how we had been delayed by Arpad, and about the long weary journey, and how we had been caught in the woods just before the storm broke. "Come, I'll show you where we spent the night." We ran ahead of him, and soon stood under the oak where we had built our nest of branches.

He wanted to hear everything, and still explaining and enjoying to the full this appreciative grown-up audience, we took him to where we had found the dead boar. We wanted to pretend we had killed it, but he was so honest and open himself, that we felt him a real comrade, so we even told him every detail of our "capture" of the boar.

Count Redey was enjoying himself, and he chuckled as we

returned to our camp. "I'd like to buy the eagle from you," he said. "I have a fine collection of birds at my castle—"

"Your castle?" Arpad looked at him accusingly. "You mean your master's castle!" We did not think it quite fair when we had told our story so truthfully that the older man should continue to try and fool us. "And we couldn't sell our eagle."

He saw there was no chance for compromise. "Would you like to go with me and see Count Redey's birds, and then meet the Count himself? After that you can go and visit your friend."

"Oh, yes. Certainly we would," we all shouted at once.

"Well, then get your things together and we can go in my chaise. I have left it with the horse on the road."

We packed our things with the greatest care, and joined the Count by the fallen tree. We had mounted the eagle upon a slender log, and tied its talons securely to it; two of the boys carried it, and we did not take our eyes off it for a single moment. Two others carried the tusks, and we divided the rest of the paraphernalia of our hunting trip.

Six boys and the Count were almost too much for the chaise, and the poor horse that had to pull it, but we arranged ourselves as best we could. The Count suggested that two of us, holding the eagle, should ride on the horse's back, so Istvan and I managed to mount and the others handed us the log to carry between us. The rest of them climbed into the chaise, and Count Redey began to laugh again as he saw his great crowd.

We moved slowly through the heavy mud toward the castle, passing through the village, where our appearance brought stares of amazement. Even the village dogs came after us, barking and sniffing and leaping all about the chaise.

The Count's servants, who had heard all the fuss in the village, were peering from windows and doors to see what was happening, and came out to greet us, not knowing whether to laugh at the ridiculous spectacle, or to wonder if the Count had gone crazy! Never, in all their memories, had he ever brought home any children, and here he was with half a dozen, and strangers at that, all hanging on to his chaise.

The servants offered to assist us to dismount and unload our hunting trophies and the rest of our baggage, but we refused, busying ourselves with keeping our things together and guarding them.

The Count, for all his lonely habits, knew how to play host to six hungry boys in a country house. He promptly ordered a fine breakfast to be served as quickly as possible.

He convinced us at last that our hunting things would be safe where we had piled them inside the entrance. But we must keep our eagle with us, we said. We had agreed that one of us should guard the precious bird at all times until we were ready to start homeward.

We had such a breakfast as had never before been set before our eyes. We were gay and full of jokes and laughter, and at the end of the long feast, we asked if we might not see the Count and thank him for his hospitality and show him our eagle.

"Yes, yes," he told us, "but first let us go into the garden. You want to see the collection of birds."

He took us through the court, and immediately we felt pity for the birds and said so. It was just absurd, we said, how neglected they were, and how undernourished. Some were being fed with seed that they would not normally eat. All the birds in the cages were suffering with lice. Sometimes two and three kinds of birds had been put into the same cage that in their natural state would never have lived together, and they annoyed each other, the larger torturing the smaller all day long.

We did not hesitate to place a dozen complaints against the Count and how he kept his bird collection.

Our host seemed impressed. He said he had complete charge of the birds, and he would appreciate it if we would arrange them for him. Promptly we began the task. First we cleaned the birds to rid them of the lice, which irritated them and made them unpleasant to look at. We washed their mouths, for some of them had been infected by disease.

Then we cleaned the cages, demanded alcohol for all the wires of the smaller ones, and paint for the floors of the larger. After the general cleaning we identified the birds, and divided them into cages, putting together only those of a similar nature. We gave them fresh water, and requested proper food for them. Many birds prefer wooden cages to wire ones, and if we had some slender willow withes we could make some for him, we told the Count, but that would take longer than we could stay. Immediately the Count invited us to stay over night so we could put all of the birds in good order.

We agreed to stay one more day. At dinner, which was served in the bees' house to please us, the Count ventured to ask, "How many birds would you take from my collection in exchange for your eagle?"

We stopped talking, surprised and shocked at this sudden offer, but the next instant we burst into hilarious laughter.

The Count's offer was a comical one to us. "We have five times as many birds as you," I told him, when he looked bewildered. "And all of them are much better cared for. They

are happy even in their cages. And you have the nerve to offer us your sick birds in exchange for our eagle?"

We lost control of ourselves in a second burst of laughter; our host now stood up and in an indignant voice called our attention to the fact that he was Count Redey and owner of the birds and all the estates round about, and he didn't like our impudence.

This was too much for the rest, and they burst into still louder laughter. When I saw that our host had indeed lost his patience, I said, "You see, they can't help it. They know how counts should look. We asked you before to let us see the real Count to thank him for his hospitality. Tell us where he is."

At that he abruptly left us, without another word. When he returned he was dressed in the old-fashioned regalia that is worn by Hungarian aristocrats on patriotic holidays—a richly embroidered costume, with beautiful decorations. Abashed, we rose, and I apologized to him for the things we had said, and there was no more laughing from any of us.

We went to bed thrilled with the knowledge that we had seen a real live count—an event more exciting to us than the wild boar tusks, the storm, or anything that had happened except the capture of the king eagle.

The next day it occurred to us that we had forgotten entirely our friend, Ludwig Nagy. We told the Count, whom we now treated with great respect, that we should like to see Ludwig, and that two of us could go off to tell him where we were.

"Never mind," he said. "I'll send my chaise for him. He's not much of a fellow, for I don't think he ever captured so much as a half-dying black crow, much less a live eagle, but if you want to see him you can. It's a long way to walk, and you wouldn't be back till dinner time."

We protested, but he made us see his plan was better, for

we still had many things to do among his collection of birds. So off went the chaise, and we went back to making willow cages and treating the sick birds.

We were just sitting down to our evening meal when Ludwig returned with the driver of the chaise. He was brought immediately to the dining room and stood in the doorway aghast to see us sitting so familiarly with the Count. It came to his mind at first that we had somehow tricked his aristocratic landlord.

When Count Redey saw his young tenant, who up to that time had not the slightest chance of entering these private apartments, he hurried to help him from his embarrassment. "Come in, Ludwig, come in. Your friends are telling me what a wonderful fellow you are at mathematics, but I'll bet you aren't half as good as they are at big-game hunting."

Ludwig sidled into the room finally, and took his place among us, but he hardly spoke a word all evening. The Count made us tell again the story of our adventures, and laughed as heartily as he had that first morning when we told about finding the wild boar sitting in the midst of the briar bush.

"Then we fell upon him with our sharp hatchets and chopped out his tusks with our hearts in our throats."

We hoped Ludwig would think the boar had truly been alive, and didn't bother to explain, either, and from his expression we decided that he was believing everything or nothing, in which latter case he would decide we were the biggest liars in six counties.

Although Ludwig said little, he was not too timid to eat, and it would have taken all his skill in mathematics to calculate afterwards how many cakes and apples he had eaten.

The Count invited him to stay all night with us, but he was too uneasy in this great house and soon took his leave. As for us, we were planning to go early the next morning, for we had no desire to keep our eagle too long in Vercsorog. We wanted to show the whole world our rare catch—especially our little piece of the world, Inferno Street. After Ludwig left, we immediately said good-night to the Count and went to bed, to be ready at dawn for our long journey home. The Count had promised to be up earlier than we were, in order to see us off.

He was as good as his word, and he had ordered a wagon for us. "Tell your father and mother," he said, "that you are fine visitors and good game hunters! And don't be too modest while you tell them." And he winked, for he knew that modesty was not one of our virtues.

We loaded our hatchets and lassos into the wagon, and packed our tent and the bundles of extra clothing under the seats. We worked swiftly, for now we were eager to get home and tell the rest of the family the story of our adventure, and show them the spoils.

Our excitement communicated itself to the Count, who laughed at our good-natured rivalry to get the best seat and to push the others into the worst. We found that the hardest problem was to find a place for our eagle, and we argued long over that, but the Count finally settled it for us, choosing the center of the wagon, where the huge wooden cage we had built would be in full view of all of us.

We each had a secret fear that during the long journey something dreadful would happen to it.

We were ready at last. We leaned out of the wagon and

each of us shook hands with the Count, who took both our hands in his and promised that "surely, surely" he would come to see us and our collection of birds. We told him we had had a fine time, and then the driver cracked his whip and we were off for home.

THE TRIUMPHAL MARCH

Chapter Fourteen

OUR JOURNEY home was an uproar. Everyone talked so loudly that it was difficult to understand what anyone was saying. Each had a plan for making use of the eagle, but not one would agree with another, especially on the question of who was the bird's actual owner.

In a rare moment of silence, when his small voice could be heard, Arpad declared that if he hadn't been with us we would never have spent the night in the woods, and that therefore by every law of right and reason, he was the sole owner!

Arpad's claim aroused a storm of protest among the others, and we had almost agreed that every boy should have a share, when Lucas, whose hearing was so bad that he hadn't caught a word of what we were saying, abruptly suggested—as if it were a new idea—that Arpad be the owner! This began the discussion all over again, and we were still at it when we arrived at the Koros River. It was near the noon hour, and the driver, as all drivers do, turned his horses down the bank to the water's edge for a drink.

The bridge was just opposite the mouth of Inferno Street, and while the tired horses took their drink, standing quietly in the stream up to their stomachs, I had an idea.

"Let's make a triumphal march," I suggested, "through Inferno Street, and show off our trophies." The idea took fire at once. "While the horses are resting, four of you must go and get our drums and trumpets. Find every member of the Club that you can, and tell them to bring their trumpets too. Tell them where we are waiting."

They scrambled out and were off, all but Istvan and I. It was harder than I had expected to persuade the driver to lend us the Count's horses, but when Istvan told him that I had been a herdboy on the Puszta, he gave in.

By that time the others were returning, and with them what looked like a small army. Since Mr. Christmas had been training us, our numbers had grown, and now there were almost fifty boys straggling across the bridge.

As Mr. Christmas's lieutenant, I had learned the commands, and soon I had them all in marching order. In front, in close formation, marched the drummers, and the trumpeters came next. Back of them came one of the horses, on which rode two of my brothers with the eagle. He was fastened to a log as on the first day when we took him to the Count's home. Immediately behind the horse marched two other boys carrying upon their shoulders the empty eagle cage. Behind them, the remaining troop.

With Istvan's help I fastened the two white tusks of the boar to my forehead, took one of the trumpets in my hand, and mounted the other horse to lead the parade. Istvan was to take his place at the rear, brandishing a knife and hatchet.

As soon as everyone was ready I blew upon my trumpet the order to march. Into Inferno Street went our parade. The trumpeters fairly split the air, and Aunt Juli, our old apple woman, when she heard the clamor and saw the army bearing down upon our yard, began frantically to pack away her fruit and yelled to our mother for help. Mother ran into the street, where she almost fainted at the sight.

It took me a long time to explain everything to her, for my brothers kept interrupting with details of their share in the adventures, but the story was told at last, and Gergely and Istvan trotted off to return the horses to the driver, and to bring back the rest of our luggage.

It was not easy to keep the Club members out of our yard. They all wanted to touch the tusks and to look at the eagle, but there were too many. We allowed only the musicians and the officers to remain, and to them we recounted the story from beginning to end. That night, before our father came home, he had heard many versions of our saga. The moment he caught sight of me, he cried, "What in the fiend's name have you been doing this time, boy? Where have you been, and what's all this talk of king eagles and wild boars?"

Once more I launched into the story, which had improved with each retelling. When I had finished, we presented him to the king eagle.

"This is indeed a splendid creature, sons," he said, his eyes resting on it admiringly. "But how will you feed him?"

Early the next morning, indeed, we were awakened by the shrieks of the hungry bird. Mother said, "Poor bird, poor starved thing, it must be very hungry to scream so. It breaks my heart to hear him, and we haven't money to buy enough for him to eat. I'm afraid you boys will have to let him go."

Her seriousness impressed me. I ordered a meeting in our clubhouse immediately. We decided that in some way we must raise a fund to buy meat daily. Until this could be accomplished, Mother gave us a small loan which enabled me to buy some scraps. By good bargaining, I bought a large portion of beef liver, and had the joy of seeing the king of the air gulp it down and cease his screams.

But soon he would be hungry again. Plainly, something must be done.

THE CIRCUS

Chapter Fifteen

WHILE WE had been away hunting big game, our rival club had taken it as a favorable time to arrange a circus performance, which had met with considerable success. They had earned for their treasury, which was usually empty, not less than two and a half pengoes—about a dollar.

We were jealous, until Lucas suggested that we hold a circus of our own.

All the next day we were busy painting posters and announcements. We set Saturday afternoon as the time for our performance, but we had to begin our publicity early in the week to be sure of a big crowd. Every paid-up member of the Club was requested to attend each meeting for the sake of the show. As soon as they arrived, we formed into columns and marched up and down the street. Five trumpets and three drums filled the air with advertisement, and Istvan called out in a loud sing-song, "Don't fail to see the Big Show for the Big Eagle."

Lucas led the parade bearing a placard which read:

THE EAGLE CATCHERS—BOAR KILLERS—AND BEAR MENACERS

WILL DEMONSTRATE THEIR ABILITIES

THEIR DARING AND

THE RESULT OF THEIR EXPLOITS

EVERYONE IS INVITED. COME ONE! COME ALL!

We thought we would arouse greater interest in our circus by taking our eagle with us, so we mounted him once more on his log, and Istvan and I carried him between us, spreading his wings and balancing him above our heads. Behind us marched little Arpad with the announcement:

MOTHERS, BRING YOUR LITTLE ONES

THEY ARE CRYING TO SEE OUR GREAT EAGLE!

The members of the rival club were aroused by our activity. We had no sooner left the street the third evening than they began another parade which stopped at every corner where we had displayed our signs. They carried jeering placards which read:

DO NOT HEED THE FLYING KUN!

(That was my nickname since the unsuccessful attempt to fly.)

HE WILL FALL FLAT AGAIN BEFORE YOUR EYES.

On another placard they had written:

THEY BORROWED THAT EAGLE.

THEY ARE FULL OF BLUFF AND BOLOGNEY.

Humiliated and angry, we sat in silence in the woodhouse, trying to think of some way to regain the confidence of our public, but no one had any good suggestions. The Club members went home that night disappointed.

I had a bad dream that night. I thought it was dawn, and that I was wandering in a deep wood where I met the wild boar whose tusks I had taken and worn so proudly on my head. The beast was searching through the thick woods for his lost tusks, and when we came face to face, I was wearing them. Unlucky me! At once the boar came raging at me, attacking me with violence. I picked up an enormous rock and threw it at him. In my struggle I hit my brother so hard with my fist that he awoke and defended himself, and Mother had to come to stop our fighting.

My brother went to sleep again, but I could not, and as I lay waiting for the family to waken, Mr. Christmas's old dog, Csimbok, who had spent the night in our kitchen, came into the bedroom wagging his tail and begging me to get up. Immediately my mind seized on an idea which I felt certain would be a good scheme for saving the show.

I swallowed my breakfast in one gulp, and hurried to the woodhouse. By the time my brothers came out I was busy painting a huge sign:

WE HAVE THE BIGGEST LIVING WONDER IN THE WORLD

TWIN BEASTS—HALF LION, HALF TIGER

THEY LIVE TOGETHER LIKE THE TWINS OF SIAM

WE CAUGHT THEM ALIVE, WITH BARE HANDS

YOU MAY SEE THEM IN COMFORT AT OUR COLOSSAL SHOW

WE INVITE YOU

I made the boys help me finish it, but I would not tell them what it meant for fear the secret would get out and our show would be ruined once more.

In the afternoon we paraded again through the length of Inferno Street. The butcher came out of his shop, and the housewives craned their necks. The boys could not explain what the sign meant, for they did not know themselves. Our rivals were silent before this new announcement. "A twin lion and tiger? Humph! A fake of some kind." But they were filled with a desire to see our show now, and that was what we wanted.

It was the hardest thing I ever had to do—to keep that secret until Saturday. Not even my mother could find out from me, though the boys, who were sure I must have told her, bothered her all day long with questions. Aunt Juli feared that we had some ferocious beast hidden in the woodhouse. "Your boys," she told Mother, "would catch the devil himself and keep him in chains. That's what I think."

On the morning of the Big Show an unexpected thing

happened. Our old teacher, Uncle Eszenyi, called us to come for his evening suits to be cleaned and pressed. He did his own housekeeping, but Mother took care of cleaning and pressing his clothes. He had been invited, as he always was, to attend the Fisherman's Dinner, and he loved to go in full dress. When, around lunch time, the boys came home with Uncle Eszenyi's best black broadcloth and a second-best suit, Lucas suggested that we give our show that afternoon in full dress, for, "It wouldn't do any harm," he said, "and we can announce a 'high life' performance." We greeted the suggestion enthusiastically.

Right after lunch we scurried out to the woodhouse and dipped our brushes once more into the paint pots. In the biggest letters we could get on the poster, we wrote:

WE OFFER TO THE PEOPLE OF INFERNO STREET
A HIGH LIFE PERFORMANCE.
ALL THE ACTORS WILL APPEAR IN FULL DRESS,
BUT THE AUDIENCE MAY COME BAREFOOT IF THEY WANT TO.

"High life performance!" jeered our rivals. "More faking." But they were curious enough now to pay whatever we asked, and now we wrote our final poster and sent Arpad about with it.

ENTRANCE FEES

1 CHILD—3 cents
2 CHILDREN TOGETHER—5 cents
MOTHER WITH BABY LESS THAN 6 MONTHS—4 cents
ALL OTHER ADULTS—5 cents

These prices almost caused a riot. Until that date, two cents was the highest charge for a local entertainment.

It was not difficult to slip Uncle Eszenyi's evening clothes out the back door, for Mother did not know they had been sent. It was almost impossible, however, to keep back the crowd which had come too early and was clamoring for admission. Mr. Christmas, our forceful commander, who had promised to play on the trumpet to accompany our acts, was a little late and we had hoped for some music before the curtain went up. Should we let the crowd in and lose their good will by making them wait too long? Or let them stand outside and perhaps have a lot of them go home?

Just as everything seemed hopeless, Mr. Christmas came striding along followed by his dog, Csimbok, and he was in a good mood. He arranged the musicians in place at once, and under his expert hand, they began their first song. As the music fluttered out upon the air, we opened the gate, and the crowd poured into the courtyard. They pushed forward, almost upsetting our home-made platform and benches.

The rival club boys came in a mass, headed by Chik, and they demanded their tickets in a block. They handed Lucas, who was cashier, a bank note. He had never held one before and ran to ask me whether he should take it. My experience with paper money for such a big amount was as limited as Lucas's own, but my experience with that bunch of boys made me sure this was stage money. Before we could get back to the cashier's stand, however, the gang had slipped into the yard without any tickets at all, and were all mixed up in the crowd. I was so indignant at Lucas that I sent him to join the musicians, and put Istvan in his place until the show should begin. Mr. Christmas objected to having Lucas in the band, for his deafness made him blow many a wrong note, but I had no other place on the early part of the program for him. In disgust Mr. Christmas took the trumpet away from Lucas and gave him a drum, ordering him to beat it as softly as he could.

The band had been playing its second selection when the rival club crashed the gates. Until then things had been going nicely. Now they tried to disturb the audience, hooting and calling for the show to begin.

"When's the high life performance to begin? Where are the full dress suits? We haven't seen a top hat yet. Where are they?"

The other youngsters in the crowd took up the shout. "We want full dress. We want full dress."

For fear of a riot I decided to change the order of the program and give them what they wanted. I took Lucas out of the band, and we went into the woodhouse, which we used for a dressing room. "Put on Uncle Eszenyi's suit," I ordered. It was much too large for Lucas, but we helped its fit with a large collection of pins. The second suit was almost as big for me, but I managed, by turning back the cuffs of the trousers and the long sleeves. When we appeared, the audience rocked with mirth. The clothes of our old teacher were known from end to end of Nagyvarad.

"Uncle Eszenyi the second," they shouted as Lucas walked on, and "Uncle Eszenyi the third," they yelled at me. Lucas did not quite catch what they were saying, and walked smiling to the center of the stage where he made a deep bow. I wondered how many poems it would take to get us out of this predicament if Uncle Eszenyi ever discovered what we had done, but there was no time for regrets now. I announced the next act, and the band began to play the song agreed upon for the Eagle Performance, and Lucas went back into the band.

Gergely, who was a very clever tight-rope walker, was to perform with the eagle balanced on his head. He thought it would be more effective if he should look like the circus ladies we had seen on the posters of shows, and so he had slipped a pair of bloomers out of our sister Marie's wardrobe, to take the place of a spangled skirt.

While he was dressing for this act, and the music was playing, I called Istvan to get Csimbok and come to the woodhouse. With his help I shingled one entire side of the dog with Mother's scissors. Then I painted large and small black spots on his side to make him look like a tiger. The other side with its long hair I left untouched. I took some of the hair I had cut off and matted it about that side of his neck, tying it on with string which hardly showed. I tied another bunch to the end of his tail, which I had also shaved clean of hair. When he was thus transformed, I shut him inside the big cage which we had built for the eagle. Csimbok did not seem to mind. In fact, on that hot summer day he seemed relieved to lose fifty per cent of his hot fur, not to speak of his fleas. He went quietly to sleep inside the cage, and I hurried to help Gergely dress, for I knew the audience would not be satisfied much longer with only music.

Gergely had taken off his trousers and was prancing about in Marie's embroidered bloomers. I made him sit down while I tied Mother's pincushion on top of his head. We had removed all the pins and needles, but for fear one might be left inside, I gathered up a wad of Csimbok's hair and stuffed it between Gergely's head and the cushion. We both thought that a fine idea, and he stood up to let me see if he looked all right before he went on.

At that moment we heard an unusual noise outside. The music had stopped. Everyone had turned and was staring at the gate. There I saw the last person I would have expected —Count Redey, who was keeping his promise to come and see us. Lucas, staring with the rest, had lost the rhythm of the music before the band stopped playing, and Mr. Christmas had put out his foot and nudged Lucas gently in the back, leaving a footprint in the middle of Uncle Eszenyi's black broadcloth coat. It startled Lucas more than shouting at him would have, and he jumped up with his back to the audience, who yelled delightedly, "See the smudge on the high life!"

Just as I was, in my ill-fitting garments, I hurried to greet Count Redey, inviting him to share in our entertainment. I guided him to the center of the platform and in a loud voice announced to our noisy audience that among our wonders we had the honor to present a live count. Count Redey laughed and did not seem to mind as he took the chair I found for him. Then I ran back to the woodhouse to see what was keeping Gergely. He had been so upset by the arrival of Count Redey that he had gone back into the shed. "I will not wear girl's underclothes. You'll have to get me the dress suit Lucas is wearing," he cried, so I had to rush out again to the orchestra. Lucas refused to walk through the audience again, for he knew their hoots were insulting even though he could not hear what they were saying. All I could get, therefore, was the coat. Gergely was furious, but there was not time to think about his appearance now, so I urged him to wear the

coat over the underclothes. The band repeated the cue, and
I led Gergely forward; on his head balanced the mighty eagle,
his wings spread wide, sitting on the pincushion and Csimbok's hair.

The audience applauded with such vigor that they
drowned out the music. Then the musicians began to laugh
too, so that they could not play another note. In the midst
of the loudest laughter, just as Gergely started to mount to
his place on the wire, the roar ceased, only to begin a second
later with greater vehemence.

First I looked toward the Count, hoping this merriment was not at his expense, and to my relief I saw that he was laughing too. Then I saw that Uncle Eszenyi was standing at the entrance to the yard! Wearing his old, out-moded dress suit I went to greet him. There was nothing else to do. My knees trembled so hard I thought I should never get there, and my words were barely audible as I invited him to come in. I led him to a place beside Count Redey and returned to Gergely on the platform, where I made the announcement as well as I could.

Gergely went up easily and quickly to the wire. He started out, stretched his arms to keep his balance, then as suddenly pulled them back and hastily scratched under the pincushion. There were fleas in that wad of Csimbok's hair! He tried to keep the audience from guessing that anything was wrong, but as he started again he only had to stop and scratch harder than ever.

Poor Gergely! He was nervous enough, facing Uncle Eszenyi in that gentleman's coat, and facing the Count in a girl's underclothes. Again and again he tried to pull down the coat to cover them, until Uncle Eszenyi called out, "Be careful of my clothes, young fellow. Don't fall off and spoil 'em!"

In spite of the difficulties Gergely managed to make his way across the wire three times, and the beautiful eagle did its part by stretching its wings and prancing on the pincushion. All at once, however, it must have stepped on a needle that was hidden in the stuffing; it gave a short "kalac!" and tried to fly away. At that instant, Uncle Eszenyi saw the footprint on the back of the coat, and cried, "Who has been using my coat as a door mat?"

It was all too much for Gergely. He lost his balance and came down on top of me. I tried to save our bird from being injured, and down we all went on the ground. I managed to protect the bird, and Uncle Eszenyi leapt to save his clothes. He promptly took the coats off our backs, to the delight of the audience, who stamped and clapped as he returned to his seat with the black swallowtails fluttering over his arm. This act was not on the program but it was thoroughly enjoyed.

The crowd was ready now for the next number, and they began to call, "Where are the twin beasts?"

Mr. Christmas started a new tune, and I announced that if everyone would remain in his seat the great world wonder would appear.

Silence and attention followed my announcement. Four of my brothers went with me to the woodhouse, and we soon came back, marching to the music and bearing on our shoulders the eagle cage which was covered with a black cloth.

Slowly we uncovered the cage, pulled Csimbok out, and placed him so that the audience could see but one side, the side clipped and painted with tiger spots.

"Here is the beast," I announced proudly. "This is the tiger side."

Then we lifted the dog and turned him about so the hairy side would show. "And here," I said, "as you can see, is the lion side."

My voice was not too sure as I ended. Csimbok, who had been sleeping all afternoon, took that moment to stretch, and with this gesture revealed himself to the audience. They saw the trick, and began talking loudly to one another about it.

Chik opened a burlap sack which he had been carrying ever since he entered, and pulled out a big cat, which meowed in fright. Csimbok, who hated all cats, pricked up his ears. The audience stopped talking. Csimbok wriggled away from us just as Chik tossed the cat onto the platform.

The last act was chaos, in which the dog, cat, and audience took part. The cat dodged among the benches, under the spectators' feet, and the dog tore after her, determined to catch her and kill her if he could! Mr. Christmas, who had seen with indignation what we had done to his pet, went after the dog, but Count Redey caught him and shouted in his ear, "Let him go. He'll never catch her in this world." He was laughing so heartily that Mr. Christmas could not help but join in.

And then I had to announce that the Big Show was over, and all the people went home, except our special guests, Count Redey and Uncle Eszenyi and Mr. Christmas. Mother took them indoors while we changed back to our ordinary clothes, and it may have been her good cake, or it may have been her gentle way, but when we came in no mention was made of the mishaps of the circus. Mother took Uncle Eszenyi's clothes into the kitchen to clean them and press them, and we went out into the courtyard to show the Count our collection of birds.

When the old teacher had gone home, carrying his dress suit, we counted up the proceeds from our show. We had more than twelve pengoes (about five dollars), which was a tremendous amount of money to us.

"We can keep the eagle," we shouted, racing into the house. "We have enough to feed him for a long time."

And the Count and our mother and even Mr. Christmas, who was busy shaving the other side of Csimbok, seemed almost as pleased over our success as we were.

GREATEST
OF FISHERMEN

Chapter Sixteen

ONE DAY Lucas, who had been out scouting, came running to find me. As soon as he could catch his breath, he declared that he had seen with his own eyes the biggest fish in the whole Koros River. It lay, he said, just under the bridge, where a crowd was watching eagerly for a glimpse of it.

A group of boys were in the woodhouse with me finishing the bookkeeping for our Club. Lucas's news of the big fish, which he said was as long as a man is tall, electrified the whole group. The detail that fired us most was his report that the rival club had a fisherman's license and were even now standing in line taking turns holding the only fishing pole among them.

We went into conference, and decided by unanimous vote to buy a fishing rod and line with the money we had just raised, and so carefully apportioned for the daily food of our eagle. We could not resist the desire to compete in the catching of the big fish, even though the whole town turned out for the same purpose.

The purchase of fishing tackle, even the cheapest we could find, reduced our fund for the eagle's food by two pengoes, but we spent it cheerfully, determined that the other boys should not beat our record as big game hunters—or fishermen —while we were loafing on the job.

We bought the rod, line, hooks, and all the paraphernalia from Mr. Haldeck, who advised a better and bigger set. We were certain, however, that we could do just as well with the cheapest. We settled our business with Mr. Haldeck and started out at once for the bridge. If we could catch this fish, our summer vacation would be a complete list of triumphs.

When we arrived at the foot of the bridge, we found among the other townsfolk who were gathered there Mr. Goromba. Now Mr. Goromba had the sole right of fishing in the city, and it was he who had control of licenses. One had to go to him and he would give or withhold the privilege of fishing in the Koros River.

As soon as we appeared the rival club boys called out, "Where are your fishing licenses?"

Mr. Goromba sauntered over and asked us to show our licenses, and of course we were unable to produce any. A license for a season cost two pengoes, and up to that time we had never paid it, simply because we hadn't two pengoes to spend just to fish. Whenever we had the desire to go fishing, we cast our hooks into the Koros, and if Mr. Goromba appeared on the horizon, we used our right and our left legs for a swift escape.

Now the case was different. The big fish had been seen under the bridge. Our rivals had obtained a license just to beat us and steal our glory. We decided to pay the fee for a fishing license, although our hearts were almost broken at parting with the two pengoes.

As we handed Goromba the money, he pocketed the coins and remarked sarcastically, "Well, boys, the money is in my pocket, and the fish is in the river. It's up to you to catch it."

"Don't worry. We will," Istvan replied. The rival boys burst into hoots of laughter. Lucas was so irritated by the insult that he added angrily, "We'll have it by hook or by crook!"

Our line, with its six medium-sized hooks, sank into the river, and we had nothing to do but to take turns holding the rod and to wait for the fish to bite. The two gangs of boys began to mock each other, until Mr. Goromba offered to give back our fees if we would only go home. He was as eager as any of us to catch the big fellow, and thought our noise frightened it off. But we would not go, and having once accepted our money he had no right to chase us away. So we spent the day, yelling back and forth, and quarreling with Goromba.

We caught only one medium-sized carp, but we did not mind, because the others had no better luck. Mr. Goromba had pulled out only half a dozen carp no bigger than our own, and he was the best fisherman in Nagyvarad. As darkness fell, we moved nearer to him. He protested at first, but we assured him that as soon as night came the majority of boys would leave, and then we would be very quiet.

The rival boys, however, had decided to stay until they

were either defeated or could catch the great fish themselves.

Mr. Goromba's line had twelve strong hooks, and a small float with a bell which rang when a fish tugged at the line. He would lie down, leaving his line while he rested. As for us, we had to hold ours in our hands to be ready to pull the moment we felt a bite. Goromba smoked incessantly, which drove the mosquitoes from him to us, and we found the situation almost unbearable. One by one, our boys went home, until only about half a dozen were left.

It was taken for granted that when you went fishing you had skill enough to cast your line into the water so it would not interfere with your neighbor's line, but as it grew later and later on that dark, hot night, the boys became careless. The continuous watch exhausted them, and one after another they followed Mr. Goromba's example and fell asleep on the embankment.

I sat there all alone, watching the stars and listening to the lapping of the water against the bridge, and trying to keep off the swarm of mosquitoes. About midnight I awoke Lucas by a slight kick, and asked him to hold the line for a while. Half asleep and half awake, he took the line from my hand. At the same instant, there came such a tugging that he almost lost his balance, and would have lost the line if he had not wrapped it about his fist. Fortunately I had not let go of it entirely, because we needed every ounce of our combined strength to hold the line and pull it in. We had no breath with which to call the others for help.

All day long we had had bad luck, but now we could actually glimpse the big fish thrashing about on the end of the line and fighting desperately to get away.

At last it was within reach. Lucas now woke the others with a shout, and it wasn't necessary to call them twice. They were up at once and rushed into the water to catch the fish in the shallows with their bare hands. There was a long fight, but they landed it at last, and I took out my hunter's knife to cut off the hook, which had completely vanished inside the fish. I thought the line seemed stronger than the one I had been holding, but I decided that the part of the cord that held the hooks was stronger than the rest.

The fish was about three feet long, and weighed almost fifteen pounds. It was a harcsa, famous to sportsmen throughout Europe as a splendid fighter. It had a mustache over two feet long. We couldn't kill it, so my brothers started home carrying it still alive between them.

Lucas and I were so intoxicated with our success, that we decided to cast in our line again. We were eager to go after the boys with the fish, and were so nervous and excited that we used bad tactics in casting. Our line spun through the air, and slipped quite out of our hands. We thought for a moment it was lost, but it had become tangled with Mr. Goromba's and as it went out over the water, his little bell began to ring.

The whole fishing camp had heard the disturbance as we landed the fish, but had paid no attention, for we had been noisier than that all day. Mr. Goromba had awakened, too, but he had only struck a match and relit his pipe. But now, when his bell rang, he was certain that he had caught the fish. With caution he drew his line in slowly. The tug had ceased, so he knew the big fish was not there, but there was certainly something on the end of his line.

He was right. Something was there, but that something was

our hooks and line. He began to examine his tackle and found that one of his twelve hooks was missing, cut off with a knife!

Mr. Goromba turned on us and demanded to know what we had caught. We told him we already had the big fish,

and our brothers had gone home with it. He claimed that it was his, and started after them. We tried to keep him back, but without success. He was stronger than we, and infuriated by what was, he suspected, unfair sportsmanship. Yelling like a demon, he dashed after the boys and the fish. The two of us raced behind him, determined to save our Leviathan of the deep and the bones of our brothers as well, if necessary.

When Istvan and the other boys heard the shouts of Goromba they began to run, too, and running through the dark with a slippery fish is no easy matter. They dropped it at every turn in the street, and would no sooner find it and start running when it would get away from them again. By the time Goromba caught up with them, they had no fish, and were glad of it.

"Where is it?" yelled Goromba, shaking Istvan by the shoulder.

"We don't know," he panted, honestly enough. But just at that moment, the fish gave a mighty flop on the grass and Goromba caught hold of it.

The boys had no intention of giving up their fish. They climbed onto Goromba's back and thumped him with their fists. He tried to defend himself with one hand, and hold the fish with the other. The fight might have lasted all night if two of the younger boys hadn't run for Father.

Father rushed to the scene, bringing a policeman with him. By this time one of the other fishermen who had come along to see the excitement, held up a medium-sized fish with a strong hook in its mouth. The big fish was empty of any line or hook at all. It must have swallowed the smaller fish and then coughed it up one of the times the boys dropped it.

The crowd gathered under the street lamp to examine this seven days' wonder. Luckily for us the decision of the policeman was that the smaller fish belonged to the man who had lost his hook. Mr. Goromba had to admit that the hook and line were his. Then the big fish, said the policeman, belonged to the one who had landed it.

It was with great rejoicing that we bore home our prize. As we walked gaily through the night, all at once Lucas began to chuckle. "I don't really know yet," he said, "whether we got him by hook or by crook!"

RESULTS
OF THE EXPERIMENT

Chapter Seventeen

THE DAY AFTER the feast, at which even our big family was unable to eat all the fish we had caught, Father declared in his sternest voice that there must be no more fun-making and adventuring during the remainder of the vacation. "For entertainment," he said, "go to your books."

I had won a fine book as head of my class during the past year. The title was "The Book of Inventors," and from it I learned more and more each day about the sciences which had developed the machine age. Our father was an engineer, and that was partly why I was interested in machines operated by steam.

One day, I told my brothers that I could produce a big surprise for them if they would only help me find a can that I could close tightly. Istvan suggested Mr. Haldeck's as the most likely place to find a large one. We descended upon the little shop at once, and when the proprietor saw us flocking in, he became nervous, and looked relieved when I told him all we wanted was an empty tin can as large as possible. While he was looking for it in his store room, I confided to him that we were going to produce steam under high pressure.

"What?" he demanded, straightening up and looking at me anxiously. "Steam, under high pressure? I hope you don't want to do it in my store, or anywhere near it?"

"Oh, no," I assured him. "It's to be a scientific experiment in our clubhouse."

He was willing then to talk business, and we bought a fairly good oil can from him. It made an excellent drum on the way home.

When Aunt Juli saw us returning to the woodhouse, and heard our activity inside, she too grew nervous, and tried to bribe Mother, sending her two of her finest apples and asking that she stop the noise in our shed. Mother accepted the present, but failed to stop our "study" for she was only too glad to have us busy with some amusement which kept us at home under her eye.

By the third day I was convinced by my experiments with the can that I could produce plenty of steam under pressure.

We had an alcohol lamp, and I started to heat some water in the can, the vent of which was open, but which we could close with one turn of the screw top. The water boiled, and the steam began to form. It came out of the little hole hissing like a snake.

The noise put Aunt Juli into an immediate panic, for her back was against our shed, and only a thin partition of wood divided her from us and our experiment. She sent Mother three more apples, and Mother came out to ask us what we were playing, and if we couldn't stop bothering Aunt Juli with that peculiar noise.

I agreed, and in order to soothe Aunt Juli's nerves, I closed the opening with the screw top, and turned the flame as low as possible. Then I went outside again to join the other boys who were picking up some scraps of wood to make a small paddle wheel to run by steam. I had left Lucas inside. He thought I had not noticed how low the lamp was burning, and turned it up as high as it had been before when the steam had hissed so beautifully.

He now joined the group outside the door, and we all discussed the possibility of buying the little steam engine that Mr. Haldeck had just got in from Nuremberg. If we could just get enough money to buy it, we could do all sorts of experiments with our tin can steam boiler.

Just at that moment a crashing, ripping noise split the air behind us. The boiler had exploded. In an instant the air was filled with screams, yells, and roars. For a second we could see nothing because of the fog that hung over the woodhouse and the whole yard.

As it began to clear, we heard the shrill voice of Aunt Juli crying for help, and we saw that the roof of the shed had slid forward and dropped over her, her umbrella and her apple stand. The shed was roofless. Happily no one had been in it, and all the boys were safe. We ran to save the old woman, who was yelling at the top of her lungs. She was promising all the apples and pears she expected to own in the next hundred years if we would only get her out. As the roof was lifted, and as Aunt Juli realized that her only injury was her terrible fright, she reduced her rich offers moment by moment. And when the roof finally left her free, her promised rewards became threats. She got up and felt herself all over, to be sure her old bones were still in good condition. Once satisfied that she was all right, she examined her old umbrella. It, too, had come out whole, and now she turned on us and began with all her strength to beat us about the heads with the umbrella.

We dodged about, trying to run through the crowd which had gathered when the sound of the explosion advertised an accident. Alas, there was no escape through such a throng. Mr. Christmas arrived at that moment, and when he saw what we had done to his property he was in a rage and wanted to turn us out at once.

"We have been good friends a long time," he told the sorrowful group of boys standing before the broken woodhouse, "but now we are enemies." He turned to my mother who had come out at the first upheaval. "I order you to move off my property at once. Take your dirty eagle who is continually threatening the neighbors. Take your flock of pigeons which has ruined the roof of my house. Take your hundreds of singing birds which make life unbearable with their eternal racket. Take your boys, who are such rascals that not even Inferno Street in all its history ever witnessed so many tricks as they can think up in five minutes. We'll have no more noise here, and no more explosions. I want to live in peace."

Poor Mother could do nothing but give her promise that we would move out as soon as we possibly could.

The next day, which was my father's day off, we moved into another house not far from the old one, but on another street, and it was a miserable place. We could not have our Club there, for gathering in the courtyard was strictly forbidden. Our pigeons had no chance to fly freely in the air, for we were told we must keep them always in the closed woodshed. Our little birds in their cages were piled about the close quarters, for there was no porch on the outside of the house, and if we kept them in the court the other tenants complained.

Life grew sad and dull. Reading was our only activity now, or sitting about the place moping. Our behavior had changed so profoundly that Mother, one evening after the small boys were asleep, said to my father with genuine anxiety:

"Sandor, I think our sons are too good these days. I'm afraid they are coming down with some illness. Perhaps they caught some disease moving into this new house. Don't you think we ought to have a doctor for them?"

Father shook his head. "I don't think they need a doctor. But you are right. The boys are too good. I am sorry to see it."

The next morning, soon after Father gloomily left for work, another gloomy-faced man came into our courtyard pulling an empty handcart behind him. He left it there, and climbed the stairs to our apartment. It was Mr. Christmas. There he looked about him for a moment, and then said, "I am sorry, Mrs. Finta, to see how you are forced to live since I put you out of my old house. There isn't much room for the boys' pets in this place, is there?"

"What do you want of us, Mr. Christmas?" asked Mother gently.

"My dear Mrs. Finta," and he looked greatly troubled. "I have changed my mind. Since you and your children left my house the courtyard is so quiet and abandoned that I can't stand it any longer. I feel abandoned too, and so lonely that I've come to tell you the wish that is in my heart. Will you bring your children, and all their pets and birds, and even their numerous friends, back to your old home? In the past year while I was living in the house with you I became accustomed to their noise, and they were good friends to me, the best in the world. I can't stand the lonesomeness any longer. I can't even play on my trumpet since they left. While the boys were there, everyone thought I played the trumpet to please them, but the truth is I did it for my own pleasure. Poor old Csimbok is dying of loneliness too; he misses the boys and their teasing. If you'll let me, while Mr. Finta is at work, I'll move you all back again where we were so happy."

He waited a moment, watching Mother's face, and when she smiled and nodded, he went on eagerly, "I've brought a handcart; it's down in the courtyard below. And while you were away I have had the apartment renovated. It has new ceiling beams so that the boys will have a place for gymnastics, and I have improved and enlarged the woodhouse, so the pets will have a better place. All for the same price."

We whooped for joy, we were so happy. All day we carried our belongings back to the old quarters. Mr. Christmas pulled the heavily loaded handcart with a light heart, and we pushed and pulled and mostly hindered, but all with the best intentions in the world.

When bystanders asked Mr. Christmas, "What are you doing? What sort of a landlord are you, pulling a handcart for a tenant?" he replied, "I must steal them back before sunset, for when their father comes home tonight, he might, in hurt pride, refuse to live in my house again."

Arpad waited in the little building until Father returned. On his arrival, he thought no one was there. He looked in astonishment about the empty rooms. Then Arpad jumped out of a wardrobe with a loud "Boo!"

He and Arpad walked home, and joined Mr. Christmas and the rest of us who were settling the cages into their places.

"Well, well," said Father, "we are back to Inferno Street. I can tell by the noise that the boys don't need a doctor."

"No," sighed Mother contentedly, and smiled at us all. "And here comes Aunt Juli." She waved to the old apple woman.

"I'm glad they're back," Aunt Juli said grudgingly. "Business wasn't so good while they were gone."

MR. CHRISTMAS TELLS
A STORY

Chapter Eighteen

WHEN WE were settled once more in our freshly painted and decorated apartments, we decided to organize a new Club. Soon it grew almost beyond our control, and the number of its members was legion; we no longer had any enemies strong enough to annoy us. Our organized Club had the appearance of an army, and was ready to be called into action the moment any danger appeared upon the horizon, which alas, it never did. For months now, no enemy had the courage to try us out. More than once we sent out companies of smaller boys, the weakest of our group, to annoy the big fellows who did not belong to our Club. But they tolerated the youngsters' insults rather than risk a reprisal; their feet grew cold at the very sight of our scouts, and with the disappearance of all foes we thought the world had suddenly grown perfect.

Then came the consequence of our wide-flung power; as in human history of greater importance than the annals of Inferno Street, decay set in and undermined our progress.

When our members realized that they had back of them a bold organization, and they could walk to school along Inferno Street, they began to neglect their duty toward the leaders and the best interests of the Club. More than half of the membership failed to pay their dues. This was serious, particularly on account of the big eagle, who was our emblem and had brought the Club its fame. No dues in the treasury might mean starvation for our wide-winged bird through the long winter. We five brothers and Lucas, and some of our most loyal members, decided to take any job that came our way. Every penny of the money we earned would go to feed the birds. For the eagle alone, we needed eleven pennies a day.

Father was unable to help us out, for in that winter following the Russo-Turkish war the factories were idle, and he was one of those who had lost their jobs. Mother was always ready to help us in our troubles, especially with feeding the birds, of which she was extraordinarily fond, and many times she managed to spare bits of meat which we always carried to the eagle. But that was not enough.

One evening we met in our clubhouse, and discussed every possible way to earn the eleven pennies a day to buy the eagle's food. There was Aunt Juli; she might give us a little work. The next day we offered her our services. She agreed to pay two pennies if we would clean the snow from her market stall, carry all her belongings to and from work, including all the apples and the umbrella. It was a hard job for only two pennies, but we took it.

One day I had an offer from the mother of one of my classmates. That woman was the stingiest housewife in all Nagy-varad, and never had been known to keep a kitchen maid or help of any kind longer than a single week. None of the peasant girls could stand her cruelty and injustice. Besides the mother and the son who went to school with me, there was a daughter, who seemed to me the most beautiful girl in the world. She was fourteen, just my age, and it was almost as much on her account as to feed the great eagle that I agreed to work in their kitchen for five cents a day. My principal task was the dish-washing, and I saw the dishes through a rose-colored halo, because they kept me near my beloved.

This left the younger boys with Aunt Juli's stall to take care of. The others swept snow from front steps, ran errands, and carried packages for old ladies out marketing. So busy were we that we had no time to get into any fights. Winter was gone before we knew it, and as spring came on and it was nearing St. George's Day when the willow trees put on their loveliest green dresses, we met one evening in the clubhouse. We were all gloomy, for it seemed to us that nothing good had happened for a long time. We tried to think up something really exciting to do, but not one of us had an idea.

While we were sitting there, without any light in the gloomy woodhouse, Mr. Christmas stepped over the threshold. In his honor, I ordered Lucas to light the short piece of candle which he had guarded jealously during the whole winter for such an occasion.

"Well, boys, what's the matter with you?" asked Mr. Christmas. "I never saw such gloom. You are as silent and as good as the little girls from the Nuns' school."

"Times are dull, Mr. Christmas," I replied, echoing what I had heard my father say many times that winter.

"Times dull? For a young man like you, Sandor? That's a queer thing to hear from you. When did times get so dull?"

"Our funds are gone, and we have to feed our pets, who are always hungry. And we're tired doing nothing all day except the same odd jobs to earn a few pennies. Of course, they're absolutely necessary if we want to keep our birds, but we need clothes and shoes too, and we haven't any way to get them now that Father's been out of work . . ." My voice died away pathetically.

"So! You are not satisfied with the small pennies you are able to earn even in these hard times. Well, if you aren't, why don't you try to accomplish some heroic deed? Then perhaps you could earn some big money and have a fortune."

Mr. Christmas's sarcasm was lost on us. Our interest was aroused, and instead of feeling gloomy, we all began building castles in the air with the money, although we hadn't the slightest idea where it was coming from.

"Mr. Christmas," I exclaimed in excitement, "don't you

know a way we can get hold of some *real* money easily?"

"So? You want to raise money, easy money, by some clever trick?" came the voice through the half-gloom. "Why not? I know plenty of people who have made a fortune by a clever trick. Always with some risk, of course, but the risk pays sometimes."

Our eager questions showed that we didn't mind a little risk —or worry too much about tricks, I'm afraid.

"All right," said Mr. Christmas. "I'll tell you a story which may inspire you, if you are tired of the common tasks which are set for common people."

It was always a great event when Mr. Christmas offered to tell a story. We drew our chairs closer and waited while he lit his evil-smelling pipe. After he had sucked some flame from our feeble candle and was sure the tobacco was glowing, he began.

"This," he said, "is the story of JACK REDPEPPER. In a country as old as Hungary, many things have happened. But only once in a thousand years could there be born anywhere such a tiny fellow as Jack Redpepper.

"He was a surprise not only to his mother, but to the whole country roundabout. Crowds of people came to see him in his cradle, which was made of half a nutshell and was just large enough for him.

"His mother watched him day by day with anxiety, but always with disappointment, because Jack got no larger than he had been the day he was born. He could hardly stretch one and a half inches from his toes to the top of his head. It was his ambition to measure two inches, but that ambition was never fulfilled.

"Though Jack was so small, his mother loved him just as any mother loves her son. She made him fine clothes of the brightest cloth, and watched him wherever he went. She was afraid someone might steal him, for he was a gay fellow, a good talker and jolly company.

"Jack was happy for a long time exploring the farmhouse and courtyard in which he lived, but on his twentieth birthday his mother surprised him with a splendid peacock feather for his hat. He looked handsome, he knew, in his beautiful hat with its feather five times longer than he was high, so he went out to walk in the courtyard. He went on and on, and in his pride did not notice that he had crossed the boundary of the yard. All at once he realized that he was in the field, where he soon lost all sense of direction. A great storm came up suddenly, and a strong puff of wind now caught his feathered hat and nearly blew it off.

" 'Oh dear,' he shouted at the top of his little voice, 'I am lost.'

"The wind blew harder every second, and little Jack Redpepper grew more and more weary, until, at last, a stronger gust picked him up, peacock feather and all, and carried him into a tree far away from his home.

"The tree was in a large park which belonged to a nobleman's castle. There was a magpie's nest close by with a mother magpie and her nestlings.

"The people of the castle were busy hurrying in and out, and there were many guests arriving for the wedding of the nobleman's daughter who was that day to wed a neighbor's handsome son, whom she dearly loved.

"While the bride was arranging her wedding dress, she laid her diamond engagement ring on the open window ledge. The mother magpie at once flew down and stole it for her nestlings. They began to play with the brilliant toy.

"The news came to the ears of the groom that the bride had lost the ring he had given her, and he refused to go on with the wedding till the ring was found. Great was the excitement when the guests learned the news. Soon they began to leave the castle, and the poor bride had to watch them go. There she stood, dressed in her lovely white gown and long veil, helplessly looking through the window where her ring had lain.

"Jack saw it all from his high perch under the nest, and decided he must help the troubled bride. Now the nestlings were quiet and the mother had flown away in search of other prey, so Jack came out of his hiding place and jumped into the nest where the young birds were playing with the ring. Like a spark he jumped among them, quickly seized the ring, and picking up two large feathers which had fallen from the mother's back, he floated away with one under each arm. Before the nestlings could recover from their surprise, Jack had glided downward to the bride's room, where she stood at the window weeping, and landed beside her.

"The girl wiped away her tears at once, and asked Jack where he had got her ring, and who he was, so small and yet so clever.

"Jack told her of his adventure, and she sent her servants to the groom to say that the ring was found and the wedding could take place. All the

guests returned, and with the ring on her finger, the bride went down to marry her beloved. The celebration lasted a long time, and Jack Redpepper was the most honored guest. When it was over, the nobleman sent him home with a rich present for his mother, a bag of gold coins.

"Not long after this, Jack told his mother that he wanted a pair of spurs for his boots.

" 'Why, Jack, what a strange wish,' cried his mother. 'Now what would you do with a pair of spurs?'

" 'Well, mother, I want to be safe, and spurs on my boots will jingle with every step and anyone passing will know where I am.'

"So Jack's mother consented, and he went at once to visit the dwarfs who lived in the neighborhood of the farm house, at the edge of a large swamp. They had always made Jack's boots, because no one else was able to make any small enough to fit his feet. The cave of the dwarfs was hollowed out beneath a large old willow tree. There they had skillfully arranged their workshop among the tree's winding roots. Roots made their doorstep, and roots made a ladder. The only light they had filtered in through these same roots.

"The dwarfs had lived in that spot for many, many years. The people in that part of Hungary knew little about them except that they were peaceful, cheerful little persons. They were especially happy if they had plenty of work. Their customers were the peasants who lived in that section. For them the dwarfs had made baby shoes, only baby shoes and nothing else, since time immemorial. The peasants would leave old shoes for repair at the foot of the willow, and when they came back next day, the shoes would be lying in the same place, all mended. Then the peasants would take up the shoes and leave the money to pay for them.

"Jack saw no dwarf outside the cave, so he stepped down the ladder with great boldness, from root to root, and finally reached the center of the circle where the dwarfs were busy at their work. He greeted them in a loud gay voice.

"The dwarfs were startled almost out of their wits, for until then they had never had a visitor. They stopped their work and gathered around Jack in amazement. He was standing beside a pile of baby shoes, and when they saw how much smaller Jack was than any of the shoes, they knew him for the person for whom they had filled several orders for tiny, tiny boots. It pleased them to find a man smaller than themselves.

"Peti, the head of the dwarfs, who was very old, put down his hammer and awl and asked what Jack wished of them.

"Jack said, 'A pair of spurs, silver spurs to jingle on my boots!'

"When Peti had measured the heel of Jack's boot he looked solemnly at him. 'I have figured it all out, my big boy, and it will be a most difficult job, a most difficult job. We can do it, though, if you can afford the price, which is a piece of gold.'

" 'Well,' said Jack, 'you shall have the gold if the silver spurs are perfect in all details. I will go now and get the coin.'

"It was easier for Jack Redpepper to promise the piece of gold than to bring the heavy coin to the cave. He was intelligent, though, and he soon invented a way of getting it there. Setting it up on edge, he rolled it before him until he reached the gnarled old tree, where Peti eagerly awaited him. The dwarf took the coin, and promised Jack the spurs very soon.

"Jack went away happy, but as the days passed he grew so curious to see the work that was being done upon his silver spurs that he went once more to the dwarfs' grotto. As he approached the willow, he heard no sounds of work, and no one replied to his shouts. Then he climbed down the root ladder into the cave, and found the dwarfs idle, sitting in a gloomy circle.

" 'Somebody has stolen the precious piece of gold,' they told him sorrowfully.

" 'What? What did you say?' shouted Jack Redpepper. 'Tell me about it.'

"Then Peti told the sad story of the dwarfs. 'Once,' said Peti, 'we dwarfs were giants, but in a mighty combat which we fought for the fairy Delibab, we were defeated. By the charm of an ugly old witch we were shrunk from gigantic size to our present pygmy form, and were forced to retreat here.

" 'The wicked giants, who had won the battle by unfair means, are jealous of the power they hold under Delibab, and they know that they are safe so long as we are under the witch's spell. But the witch said that we could secure our release if we would pay her twelve times our weight in precious metal.'

"Jack understood, as he listened, why the dwarfs were always so busy, and why they asked for gold and silver pieces as pay for their services.

" 'You see,' continued Peti, 'why we are so upset. The other day we cleaned and shined the big coin which you brought in payment for the silver spurs, and left it to dry in the sun. It was unguarded for only an instant, but that was long enough for some clever thief to steal the biggest piece of precious metal we ever earned. We are broken-hearted.'

" 'Did you see anyone near the spot where you placed the coin?' Jack asked of Peti.

" 'No . . . no . . .' replied Peti slowly. 'No man would be able to enter the place where we had our treasure. A bird might, but no person at all.'

"The moment Peti said the word 'bird,' Jack Redpepper straightened up. It was clear to him that the thief who had stolen the shining metal coin was none other than the mother magpie who had stolen the diamond ring from the nobleman's daughter.

" 'Do you not be sad, good Peti. I know the thief, and you may be sure we shall get back our gold coin, and perhaps others besides!'

"The day after that conversation Jack Redpepper rolled another large gold coin to the cave of the dwarfs. This they also shined and placed in the same spot from which the first coin had been stolen. With the aid of the dwarfs, Jack laid a trap for the thief. With a sheet of paper he formed a small cone, and covered the inner side with glue from the gluepot which the dwarfs used in their shoe repairing. The cone was sunk into the ground, and the gold piece placed inside it.

" 'Now,' said Jack, 'we must hide ourselves in the bushes and wait.'

"It was not long before they saw the shadow of a bird flit across the place. Jack looked up and recognized the mother magpie. He signaled the dwarfs to keep very quiet.

"The moment the magpie spied the newly burnished gold piece, she flew down slowly, with the greatest caution. Flitting from bush to bush and chirping as though she had nothing serious on her mind, she came at last to the clearing and the piece of gold. Down went her bill into the cone, the glue stuck her fast, and there she stood, with her head buried, until the dwarfs gathered about her and bound her wings and legs.

"When they had carried her into their grotto, they chained her to a strong root beside their work bench and undid the other cords which bound her. At once the clever magpie tried trickery. 'Oh, you are such good-hearted fellows,' she said. 'You will believe me when I tell you that all I wanted to pick up that coin for was to learn the shape and date of it. I have no need of money. We magpies have plenty of gold hidden away in a secret place. My fledglings are just out of the nest today,' she continued sadly, 'and I am afraid they will get into mischief while I am gone. O good dwarfs, let me go.'

"When the dwarfs heard mention of a hidden treasure, their eyes began to shine. They glanced at each other with deep understanding. Jack Redpepper had been right; they would get back the gold coin which he had paid them for the spurs, and perhaps many others besides.

" 'Tell us, what do you think we ought to do next?' they begged of Jack, and he gathered them at the other end of the grotto where the mother magpie could not hear, and told them his plan.

"The next day, the dwarfs set up their trap with the gold coin once more. The young magpies, who could now fly well, became anxious when their mother did not return to the nest, and decided to go out and search for her. There were five of them, and they went in five different directions.

"It was the youngest who flew in the direction of the dwarfs' cave. The moment he saw the shining metal he forgot his mother, and flew down to see what glittered so in the sun. One peck at the coin, and he was caught in the same manner as his mother.

"The dwarfs bound him too, and then told him that his mother had been captured, and that she would be kept prisoner until her relatives were willing to unite their forces and bring the dwarfs all the precious metal they could assemble—all that they had ever stolen.

"When the dwarfs took the magpie to his mother, she begged her son to do whatever they asked to buy her liberty again. Then they let the young magpie go free.

"The young magpie convinced his family that this was the only thing they could do, and soon even the oldest was carrying his entire treasure to the cave of the dwarfs under the gnarled old willow.

"Jack Redpepper made a scale for weighing the gold; it was an empty basket on one end of a long pole, which lay across a log, and on the other end of the pole sat one of the dwarfs.

"As a flock of magpies appeared bringing their gold and silver, they flew over the basket and dropped in the precious objects—spoons, forks, rings, and jewels of all shapes and sizes. Jack Redpepper stood in the center of the improvised scale and watched until the weight of the metal exactly balanced the weight of the dwarf.

"For three days and three nights, a cloud of magpies hung over the basket, filling it with treasure. The little dwarfs toiled busily, storing away the precious hoard. On the fourth day, the magpies settled about the grotto, and the eldest one said, 'We are very weary now, and we have brought you all we possess. Now let the mother magpie go.'

"The dwarfs counted and recounted their store, and knew that the time of their ransom had come. They no longer had any reason to keep their prisoner, so they released her, and all the magpies flew away. Then the dwarfs turned gratefully to their deliverer.

" 'Here are your silver spurs, and the two gold pieces besides. We do not need them now, for we can buy our ransom from the old witch with what we have, and we shall be free again. But we shall always remember you as the best friend the dwarfs ever had.'

"Jack Redpepper went home to his mother's farm, jingling his fine silver spurs, and rolling the two heavy gold coins before him. His heart was light, for he knew that the dwarfs would now be released from their enchantment, and would return to their home in the land of the beautiful fairy, Delibab, where they would live forever and ever."

◦§ ໄ◦

When Mr. Christmas had finished the story of Jack Redpepper, he left us without so much as a "goodbye." We sat for a while in silence, thinking of all the gold which the magpies must have hidden since the days when Jack Redpepper was alive. One by one our friends left the woodhouse, and nothing was left for us to do but go to bed. I doubt if any of the boys slept that night without dreaming of wild and curious ways of following in the tiny footsteps of little Jack Redpepper.

THE BARGAIN

Chapter Nineteen

THE NEXT NIGHT we were in the midst of a long argument regarding little men and big fortunes, and discussing the meaning of Jack Redpepper's story, when Mr. Christmas appeared.

He took his seat on an up-ended log, and began to smoke and talk. "I forgot to finish my tale yesterday," he began. "I was in too much of a hurry to get away. One little thing I forgot to mention. Before the dwarfs stepped on the scale invented by Jack Redpepper, they made themselves heavier by filling their pockets with sand, and in that way gained more of the precious metal than was necessary for their ransom. Dwarfs are very cautious creatures by nature. They feared another enchantment might change them into dwarfs once more, and so they wanted to be prepared by having sufficient gold hidden away to buy their freedom again. Never since, however, have they needed their hidden gold, and the treasure still lies at the foot of the willow trees which grew near the ruined fortress of Bihar. You know the spot, for it is not far from Nagyvarad. The trees were once called weeping willows, but now the folk roundabout call them laughing willows, because guarding the treasure of the dwarfs through so many years has changed their natures.

"People do say that on St. George's Night, which is only a few nights off, those same trees burst into flame at midnight, to show under which ones the treasure is hidden. Midnight is the witch's hour, you know."

The old man could scarcely finish his sentence, so eagerly did we break in with a thousand questions. He gave his answers to them all. At last we asked, "Will you be our guide to the ruined castle?"

"Why not? If you will pay for my services . . ."

Pay for his services? We were ready to offer any salary he might want. "How much?" we demanded eagerly.

"Just one hundred pennies," said Mr. Christmas. "And for these pennies, I shall teach you the secrets necessary to gain power over the treasure, and protect you from the witches who are jealous of anyone seeking to carry off the gold."

I almost tumbled off my chair when I heard that for this generous service Mr. Christmas wanted only a hundred little pennies.

"How can you do all that for such a little bit of money?" I asked in surprise.

His voice was amused. "Yes, it is a little bit of money, son, but it must be paid *in advance!*"

We immediately broke into protest, because we hadn't a red cent to our names.

"I'm sorry," answered Mr. Christmas cheerfully. "You will have to work hard, then, in the next two days, if you want to hunt for the gold on St. George's Night. If you let this opportunity go by, remember you will have to wait a whole year before you will have another."

When he had left us, we talked things over. We could not call in the help of our numerous members, for we wanted to have the whole treasure to divide among ourselves.

The two days that followed were most strenuous. We had to earn one hundred pennies, and all at once it seemed that every penny had vanished from the face of the earth. From early morning till late at night we were engaged in all kinds of activity. We offered our services in every place where there was the least likelihood of a penny. We were ready to do work which before would have insulted our dignity. We offered everything we had—knives, balls, pets, everything except our collection of birds—for such low prices that the other boys thought us crazy. But no one had any money to buy.

In spite of all our zeal, at the close of the second day we found we were short twenty-four cents. Our only hope seemed to be to win the confidence of Aunt Juli, which wasn't easy, for she had never trusted us with more than one apple in advance of our ability to pay. Now it was not apples we wanted, but twenty-four of her hard-earned pennies. It was almost too much, to humble our pride before Aunt Juli. But we were the far-famed hunters, and so . . .

I borrowed Mother's broom and began to sweep about Aunt Juli's stand. She stared at me in wonder and asked in her shrill voice, "Boy, have you gone crazy now for sure? Here it is late in the evening, and just when I want you to help me home with my belongings you get a notion to clean my stall. What a foolish lot you are!"

Aunt Juli was sensitive about the cleanliness of her place on our sidewalk, and I had thought to please her with this activity. It almost broke my heart to see that she didn't appreciate it. But I did not lose my nerve.

"You see, dear Aunt Juli," I began, "we are in terrible trouble today. We need fifty pennies more than we ever needed anything in our lives. We should appreciate it if you would lend us that little money, or give it to us as an advance for our good services in the near future."

I thought it was an elegant speech, but Aunt Juli threw back her head and laughed. "Boy," she chuckled, shaking her head, "you will give me apoplexy. Half a hundred pennies! In advance! And what would happen if you should die? Who would be responsible for your debt? Tell me that."

"We are too young to die soon, Aunt Juli. It isn't likely old age will take us before we pay you back. And you know that of all the seven brothers in our family, one will surely live to pay back every penny you lend us."

My seriousness and sincerity impressed Aunt Juli, and she looked about into the ring of anxious faces. We were all young, and healthy, and her best customers.

After several long minutes, Aunt Juli broke the silence. "If you are really in as urgent need of money as you say, I will lend you twenty-five cents and no more, on the condition that until you pay me back every cent, you will not blow your trumpet or beat your drum, and you will not try any more blasting experiments in the woodshed just behind me."

We had judged Aunt Juli correctly in asking for fifty cents; by giving us just half of that she was meeting our need. The twenty-five pennies were counted into my palm, and immediately we opened a new piece of bargaining—to buy a two-cent apple with that one superfluous cent. It was a double victory. We cut the apple into six parts and divided them among those who were in on the responsibility of the treasure hunt, and we faced the meeting with Mr. Christmas that evening with light hearts.

RULES FOR
FINDING THE TREASURE

Chapter Twenty

MR. CHRISTMAS was as cautious in business as Aunt Juli had been. He counted the hundred pennies three times before he dropped them into his pocket. "Better a sparrow today," he said, "than a bustard tomorrow." His philosophy puzzled us slightly, but we were impatient to learn the rules for hunting the treasure and quickly forgot everything else.

As usual, Mr. Christmas first fixed his pipe, and when it was glowing well, he began to talk.

"First," he said, "you must find the crossroad nearest the spot where the laughing willow trees are blooming.

"Second, you will have to draw a magic circle about the crossroad, which circle will defend you from every attack of the witches who jealously guard the hidden treasures, and who will try to drive you away from that point of safety. The circle must be drawn with a mixture of bat's blood and lime, and you must use a crow's wing to paint it, walking backwards and using your left hand. Be careful not to close the ring, but arrange a broom across the opening as a door which you may use as an exit for leaving the ring, but which the witches cannot use as long as the broom is there.

"Third, you must not talk in words all the time you are in the ring, though you may use some sign language. You will have to invent one before tomorrow evening.

"Fourth, if you want to move about the ring, you must not stand up, but move about like dogs with one hurt paw."

"We don't quite understand," I told him.

"This way," he explained. "Move about on your legs and one arm, holding up the other arm to point in the direction in which you want to move."

"Oh, that's easy," we all cried.

"Easy? Yes, it's all very easy," growled our friend. "But don't forget the fifth rule. In case of danger, if you are hurt or feel any pain anywhere, you can relieve it by whistling backwards. Shut your teeth this way"—and he showed us how—"and then draw your breath back, making a shrill noise. Of course none of you will whistle from fright, only if you are really hurt. And should you find the pain more than you can bear, try to make a circle by revolving your hand above your head at the same time that you make a vertical line over your stomach with the other hand. But be careful not to get the two moves mixed, and do them at the same time or trouble will follow. That formula is known as the pain-expeller."

Sitting in a ring about our instructor we tried to follow this formula. At first we found it difficult, but soon we were experts at it, some with the left hand over the head and some with the right, and all with the opposite hand over the stomach.

Clicking the pennies in his pocket, Mr. Christmas left us to think over his instructions. As he went out he tossed over his shoulder a final word. "Do not by any chance step over the mark of the ring. Otherwise, the charm will be broken."

"Goodbye," we called after him, "and thanks."

The next day was St. George's Day. It took the six of us half a day to find one lone sleepy bat. Arpad had less trouble bring-

ing in a crow. Then we mixed the magic paint and had it ready with our brush to paint the charmed circle.

As the time approached for Mr. Christmas to come for us, we looked over our paraphernalia and decided that everything was in readiness. We had collected seven empty sacks for carrying home the treasure, and we had some food, our hunting knives, hatchets for the stubborn roots of the willow trees, and shovels for digging the earth that covered our riches. The moon had risen and the hour was late when our guide arrived.

As we reached the open road connecting the village of Bihar with the city of Nagyvarad, we couldn't resist the temptation to give vent to our high spirits with shouts and yells. Uncle Christmas only smoked and smiled. Then, as we went the four miles between Nagyvarad and Bihar he told us the history connected with the country we were traveling through, an inspiring story which only convinced us that our own adventure would have a brilliant end.

Arpad, the founder of Hungary, had a fierce enemy in the chief of the Bulgars, named Men-Maroth, who, to stop the advance of Arpad and his Magyars, had built earthworks on the boundary of Transylvania, which at that time was called Dacia.

Men-Maroth thought that the Magyars, who fought only on horseback, would be unable to conquer his fortress of earth at Bihar, so he kept only a small company with him to defend it and sent the main body of his army elsewhere to move around the flank of the Magyar army and come upon them from the rear. When the fortress was besieged by the Magyars, they offered a duel between the two warlords, which the Bulgars accepted, and in the fight, Arpad killed Men-Maroth and dispersed his army. The fortress was soon abandoned, and centuries of weather had leveled it to the earth.

The Turks had used that same fortress many times during the long years when they occupied Hungarian territory. They, too, buried their treasures there, for in the fierce onslaught of the Hungarians, they had been unable to take their possessions with them.

Keeping up with Mr. Christmas, listening to every word that fell from his lips, we forgot the passing time and the weariness of our long journey. Then abruptly he stopped and pointed to the horizon.

"There," he said, "is your destination. There is the ruined fortress, and around it are the ancient willow trees."

The moon had reached her zenith, but clouds had darkened her brilliance so that we had to strain our eyes to see the gnarled and twisted trees, and the low mounds of the ruin.

"Before the moon is entirely clouded over," said our guide, "we ought to make a short cut through that cemetery which lies here to the left of us."

When Mr. Christmas suggested that we cross through the cemetery at that time of night, we all looked hesitant, but we were under his orders, and raised no objections.

We had hardly entered the gate of the cemetery when the word "Halt!" rang in our ears. It was only Mr. Christmas, but it might have been a voice from one of the graves, it frightened us so. We drew together and looked about us fearfully.

"There it is!" said Mr. Christmas, pointing, and speaking in a trembling voice unlike any he had ever used before. "There's a black cat crossing our path. That means bad luck for all treasure hunters! But maybe you will be an exception."

In the dark we turned to where he pointed, and even today I am not sure whether there was a black cat there or not.

When we had arrived at about the center of the old cemetery, a flock of crows flew over, circling and cawing. Mr. Christmas stopped us again, and threw back his head to watch the movement of the birds. Then he asked with suspicion in his voice, "Has any one of you killed a black crow lately?"

"Yes, Uncle. You know you told us we had to have one wing for a paint brush for the magic circle, and Arpad killed that crow just today."

"Too bad, too bad! You should have had someone else do it for you." He shook his head reprovingly. "I hope you had somebody else catch the bat? You didn't kill any today?"

I had no time to reply, for at that moment a bat swooped so close that I thought he would knock off my hat. How I wished we had not been so selfish as to keep every other member of the Club out of this enterprise. We walked in a single line between the rotting crosses of wood that marked each grave, watching right and left wherever our guide called our attention to shadows in a fearsome voice like nothing he had ever used before. When we had left the graveyard and its crosses, and its bent and twisted trees that gave reality to the ghosts that Mr. Christmas would have had us see, we breathed more easily, and drew apart, for we had almost tramped on the fellow next to us in our eagerness to stay close together.

"It's most important now," our adviser said in his more natural voice, "that before the moon goes down we find the crossroad for your observations."

None of us wanted to find it immediately, for we knew that when we did Mr. Christmas would leave us, and somehow we

were eager for his company just then. But before very long he
halted us at a spot where two narrow lanes crossed.

"Here," he said, "is where we part. My share in the work is
done. I am happy to leave this place, where so many people
have tried to repair their fortunes, and where a few have indeed come back with treasure and some with whole skins."

This farewell was not encouraging, not a bit, and when we
urged Mr. Christmas to remain with us a while longer, he
refused in the same manner, saying he had no taste for adventure which depended upon witches' tricks.

"It's all right for you," he declared, "you are young and
brave. But now don't waste any more time in discussion. Arrange your magic circle as large as possible to protect your
health, your humor, and . . . well, your life. Maybe . . .
well, I won't make you uneasy at this late date." And with a
brusque "Goodbye, big-game hunters," he left us.

WHEN GHOSTS ARE WALKING

Chapter Twenty-one

 FOR THE FIRST time in my life I had
no voice in my throat with which to say farewell to Mr. Christmas. When he was gone, however, it was
up to me to keep a brave front, for all the rest were younger
than I, and it would not do for me to show fear.

Therefore, as Mr. Christmas disappeared into the darkness, I said to my brothers, "Poor Mr. Christmas, it's no wonder he never became rich, and has only two or three little old apartment houses, when he hasn't courage enough to share a simple adventure like this."

The boys nodded their heads, but it seemed to me they weren't so sure he wasn't wiser than we. Lucas, however, who hadn't heard much of the conversation, put down the broom he had been carrying and urged me to action.

There was still a faint glimmer of the moon, and by the light of it we tried again and again to make a good-sized circle in the center of the crossroads, but the most we could shape it was about fifteen feet in diameter. This worried us, for we saw that we should have little room to move about, when seven boys were inside. "Well, anyway, we'll be close enough to protect one another," said Lucas, marking where the painted circle must go to meet the handle of his broom.

That idea quieted the boys' jumpy nerves, and while Lucas and I painted the magic ring with the bat's blood and lime, they practiced the sign language, which we had made up that afternoon. We had made it short, simple, and easy to remember. It went as follows:

A pull on the nose: *Look this way*

A touch on the right ear: *Enemy in sight*

A touch on the left ear: *Enemy gone*

Open palm: *No danger*

Closed fist: *Keep quiet*

Closed fist, one finger out: *You can move*

A thump on another's chest: *Get out and run as fast as you can go*

We thought that would answer any emergency that might come up.

We used every drop of the mixture and painted as wide a line as we possibly could, but it faded in the dark. It seemed as if Lucas spent a long time placing the broom. Then one by one we filed into the ring through the broom door, and closed it with gloomy forebodings.

Once inside, we were under the spell of the ring and must not speak again; all we had was our limited sign language, and I found it almost impossible to use the signs to make the boys take their places within the circle. They shook their heads, and tried to push others to the outside, and it wasn't until I sat each one forcibly in his place that order was restored.

Crouching upon our empty sacks, we waited in bewildered silence for what would happen next. We turned our heads this way and that. All we could see was the black outline of the willow trees, which seemed to change their shape constantly, and move like phantoms.

It was a beautifully cool night, but we perspired like stokers in an engine room. Crouching for so long, our legs grew stiff and began to ache. The boys would stretch first one and then the other, and fidget against me till I was so nervous I couldn't keep a good lookout. They only stopped when I pulled Lucas's and Arpad's noses, and pointed upward to a flock of bats circling over us.

Gergely, who had killed the bat, grew uneasy, and edging toward me on three legs, he pointed toward the center of the ring. I replied with a closed fist and one finger out, which meant that he could move, for I knew he had a right to worry at that moment. But Arpad, who up to that time had been fairly comfortable in the center of the ring, didn't want to leave his position. Immediately a new controversy began, in which all took part, mostly to show that they could use the sign language, but also to take their minds off our uneasy situation. The controversy ended suddenly. Istvan gave me a terrible blow in the back below my ribs, which wasn't in our code, but which made me turn and look without considering what it might mean. In that instant all of us pressed into the very center of our magic ring, so tightly wedged that I could not draw a full breath. Between the old willow trees a white form appeared. We were motionless, but our hearts leapt into our throats and stayed there, beating like clocks gone crazy. The smaller boys would have run at once, if we had not held them firmly by the coat-tails. But I did not feel the brave commander I ought to have been, for every inch of my body began to tremble and my courage oozed out of my toes. I wished I might shout to the boys, "Get out of here," but my tongue stuck between my teeth. As for the sign language, my arms were too stiff at my sides to lift, and all I could do was sit and watch the apparition come nearer and nearer.

Then it turned, as if it had not seen us, and moved away along the embankment of the ruined fortress just behind the willow trees. Each of the boys breathed deeply and began pulling his neighbor's left ear, which meant "enemy gone," but we were too ready to hope. The ghost wheeled about, and running down the embankment, made straight for the circle before any of us could signal with a closed fist or a tug on the right ear!

The ghost drew up sharply just outside our magic circle as if it had struck a stone wall. It staggered about there, wav-

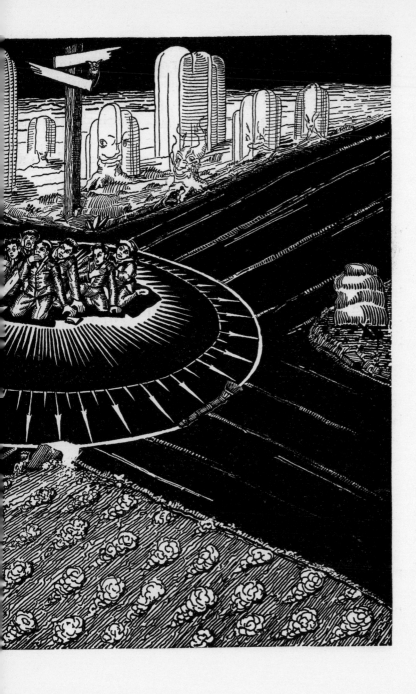

ing its white arms, and seeming every instant about to topple forward on top of us. But the magic of our invisible wall kept it out. It tried to find some break, but apparently had no power to enter the ring, which made the ring seem to us a wonderful stronghold.

The ghost moved off a little way and ran at the circle from another angle, but brought up against the wall as sharply as before. Again and again it tried. Then it came upon the broom at the doorway. Our hearts leapt again in an agony of fear that Lucas had not matched the ends of the broom exactly with the ends of the circle. As a coil for electric current is useless if there is a tiny break in it, we knew our ring to be useless if Lucas had not made close contacts. What we went through while that ghost like an engineer examined every inch of that dirty old broom! It gave a second and third examination, and then waving its tunic with anger, floated away toward the silent cemetery.

Such a lifting of the strain on us! Each of the boys was eager to describe how he had felt under the danger, but the sign language was not very flexible. I could only repeat "enemy gone" and "no danger" and "you can move." In my heart I wondered if we were indeed finished with that ghost.

The others were more optimistic. They made fancy gesticulations, even trying to joke in the sign language. They almost stretched their legs out of the ring, making up funny dance steps on three legs, and doing a Russian folkstep. Oh, they were full of fun once they were convinced that nothing could penetrate our magic circle!

But my worry had not been groundless. The gaiety was put to an abrupt end by a noise from a clump of bushes very

near us. It was the ghost. It paused again on top of the embankment, skirting the path about twenty feet above us,
and stood so long that we almost fell asleep watching. It must
have stayed half an hour. When it finally started forward, I
almost sighed with relief. This time, from the door of our
circle it waved a long stick, in the same way that a fisherman
might cast with his rod. Indeed, the ghost must have been
the wandering soul of a deceased fisherman, for after a while,
very slowly, it lifted the stick and we saw a white line dangling
at the end. Evidently, since the ghost could not get into our
magic ring, it had decided to fish for us over the wall. It cast
its line again and again, but always the hook dangled just
above our heads. It would pull the line out slowly, and examine
the end. And during that pause we would be waiting in terror
for the line to descend above us once more, until we were
driven almost to the point of insanity. Then, with no sign
this time of disappointment or annoyance, the ghost moved
off and vanished once more into the darkness.

No gay mood followed this time. The boys were too disheartened even to stretch their cramped legs. They gave the
sign to leave, before something more should happen. A single
move on my part would have taken them through the broom
door, and they did almost bolt when we heard a terrible noise
in the direction of the cemetery as the ghost came crashing
back through the bushes. This time it carried two long sticks
and at once began to poke at each one of us, dodging rapidly
here and there about the circle until the boys were in a frenzy.
We could bear it no longer, and we hadn't courage enough to
run through the door. But I remembered that we might move
about on three legs like an injured dog. As the ghost came near

me I tried this, but when I assumed the three-legged posture lifting high that part of my body on which I had been sitting till then, the ghost's second stick fell with a swishing and a loud ker-whang, and I collapsed. The other boys began to mill about on three legs, only to be beaten in their turn. There rose a chorus of hissing whistles as the rules had ordered, but the rules were quickly forgotten and the hisses went uncontrolled in or out as our fright or pain suggested.

The cruel ghost would prod us, and prod, until in desperation a boy would scramble away only to feel the thud of that second stick which was growing surer in its aim with practice. We huddled now in the middle of the ring and each of us tried the "pain-expeller" movement we had practiced. In the woodhouse we had done it with such ease! Now we made the circle over our heads with the wrong hand, and the vertical lines over our stomachs were wobbly, and the pain did not cease. I used all possible combinations of circles and vertical lines, and still the pain burned where I sat. Then I tried making circles in that spot, and when the boys saw my new pain-expeller, they rubbed themselves with equal vigor. But the moment they exposed any inch of their anatomy, prod went one stick, bang came down the other, until we thought we saw stars, rather than flames, on the willow trees about our ring.

Whistling inwardly did no good; the pain expeller was useless. Lucas solved the problem by falling face down on the ground and beginning a loud roar. The other boys might have followed his example if at that moment the ghost had not in a delighted trot run toward our door and begun dashing the broom to pieces with his stick. As the broom fell apart, we saw that the magic of the ring had been destroyed by Lucas's cry.

I leapt to my feet, calling "Run!" and grabbing the sacks and shovels we tore for the village of Bihar.

It is without shame that I confess I did not choose the short cut through the cemetery. Even in our mad rush we took the long way round. Behind us we thought we heard the flapping garments of the ghost, and we ran faster. I grabbed Arpad's and Lucas's hands, and they in turn grabbed hold of the other boys, and so we raced toward the village streets at that hour of the morning, while all good folks slept.

We had forgotten our bruises, our aches. I looked behind, and saw the ghost only a stick's length away.

"At the edge of the village it must stop," I panted, trying to put heart into my brothers.

But a ghost as valiant as ours was not to be deterred by a few houses and rambling streets. It came on, clattering its stick along the palings of the fences with such vehemence that every dog in the village came barking at our heels.

I never remembered how we left the village and once more gained the open country. But the barking died away, and when I looked again we had lost our ghost. When we slowed our pace we found that we had lost everything along the way —our shovels, our hatchets, even our hats. All we had clung to was the sacks, the seven empty sacks. Our pace was slow. We had no desire to talk. At the bend of the road we saw the dark figure of a man seated upon the embankment. This was a new terror, we thought, and we stepped hesitantly forward. There was no going back to Bihar, with its infuriated dogs and its ghost.

The boys pressed closer about me, until with relief we heard the cheerful voice of Mr. Christmas calling, "Hello, treasure hunters! Back so soon? What have you in your sacks? I thought I might as well wait here till you came along."

We stared at him glumly and no one spoke.

"Come, come. Tell me, haven't you anything to show for the night's work?"

We shook our heads without a word.

"Can't you tell me why you failed, then? I gave you the rules."

"I don't think we feel much like talking about it, Uncle Christmas," I said. "We just want to go home."

I started ahead of the other boys, who let out an occasional exclamation of pain when a new sore spot started aching. We had not curiosity enough to ask Mr. Christmas what he carried in his well-stuffed valise that swung so casually in his long fingers. His other hand he kept in his pocket, and with it he made a fine jingle among the pennies which we had gathered with such effort and which we had sacrificed so lightly in hope of a larger treasure. One hundred real pennies for a dream of fool's gold! What idiots we had been!

I recalled the words of Mr. Christmas when he had taken the coins. "Better a sparrow today than a bustard tomorrow." I who had gone hunting bustards on the Puszta in the winters when I had been a herdboy there should have known what he meant. Yes, those hundred little pennies were sparrows which we had given too easily, and we should have no bustard tomorrow!

The moon still hung above the hills, and now the clouds parted and let her full face shine down upon us. If she saw into my heart, she knew that there was a secret resolve in it to be a big-game hunter no longer. Not for me ever again such nonsense. Next time I should be happy to count the sparrows, and let the other fools go after tomorrow's bustards.

A wind sprang up. We were chilly, and each boy drew an empty sack over his head, and so, like a company of gloomy dwarfs, we walked homeward, each thinking his own thoughts.

Lucas began to try again the gesture for pain-expelling, at which even now he made no headway. At last he remarked, "I don't know what foolish fellow ever called those old trees laughing willows. They ought to call them weeping willows the same as any others. That's what I think!"

And we all agreed with him—except, perhaps, Mr. Christmas.

The End